When someone we love is dying from a prolonged illness, the grief we experience is especially hard, because we actually grieve twice -- first when we acknowledge the potential for loss, and then again upon the person's actual death.

The anticipatory grief associated with prolonged illness and the grief that follows death can evoke many feelings, including sadness, guilt, loneliness, confusion, anger, and despair. In dealing with all of these emotions, we need support and comfort. Helping individuals cope with this difficult situation is the mission of this book.

Service Corporation International, the world's recognized leader in funeral service, recognizes the need for and importance of grief materials that help people deal with loss. In this spirit and with genuine concern for the community, SCI is committed to providing assistance, guidance, and support through a life-enhancing program it has created and underwritten entitled "Picking Up The Pieces."

Living With Grief: When Illness is Prolonged is the sixth and most recent volume of this ongoing and comprehensive program written by nationally recognized loss and bereavement experts. This public service program is available to the entire community through funeral homes and cemeteries affiliated with SCI.

The complete "Picking Up The Pieces" program includes a series of non-denominational books and videotapes with expert information and insights. In addition to *Living With Grief: When Illness is Prolonged,* other subjects include:

> *Working Through Your Grief*
> *A Child's View Of Grief*
> *Helping Children Cope With Grief - A Teacher's Guide*
> *Someone You Love Is Dying. How Do You Cope?*
> *Living With Grief: After Sudden Loss*

For additional copies or information about our "Picking Up The Pieces" program, please contact any SCI funeral home or cemetery -- or call 800-9-CARING (800-922-7464).

Living With Grief
When Illness
Is Prolonged

Edited by Kenneth J. Doka, Ph.D.
with Joyce Davidson

HFA
HOSPICE FOUNDATION OF AMERICA

Taylor & Francis
Publishers since 1798

©1997 by Hospice Foundation of America

Ordering information:

Bookstores and individuals order additional copies from
Taylor & Francis
1900 Frost Road, Suite 101
Bristol, PA 19007

To order by phone, call toll-free 1-800-821-8312
or send orders on a 24-hour telefax, 215-785-5515
Orders can be placed via Internet at bkorders@tandfpa.com

For bulk quantity orders, call Hospice Foundation of America, 1-800-854-3402

Hospice Foundation of America
2001 S Street, NW Suite 300
Washington, D.C. 20009
www.hospicefoundation.org

Typesetting and design by Edington-Rand, Inc., Riverdale MD

Hospice Foundation of America staff assistance from Lisa McGahey, Clese Erikson, Chris Procunier and Jon Radulovic

Library of Congress Cataloging-in-Print data available upon request

ISBN: 1-56032-703-0

To my Son
Michael
In Celebration of his
Transition into Adulthood

K.D.

In Memory of my Mother,
Who Taught me to
"Buy Hyacinths
To Feed the Soul"

J.D.

To Cokie Roberts,
for her Ongoing Support of
and Insights into
the Needs of the Bereaved

K.D., J.D.

Contents

Foreword

Jack D. Gordon
President, Hospice Foundation of America

This book marks the third collection of articles in our *Living With Grief* series, and augments our April 1997 teleconference dealing with grief during and after long-term illness. The book is designed to explicate some of the issues certain to be raised by the teleconference. At the same time, it will direct further consideration of the topics by all readers, whether they attend the teleconference, watch the video, or read the book.

Hospice Foundation of America started this annual teleconference series because we saw a need to educate hospice workers and volunteers about bereavement issues. There was such a strong response, one which grows stronger each year, that the scope has widened to include all those who deal with bereavement in its variety of forms. In many communities, the teleconference now serves as a meeting place for various people and agencies to learn about each other and cooperate in responding to community problems.

The hospice movement itself has grown from the establishment of the first American hospice in 1973 to over 2500 separate organizations today. This means that hospice is filling a need that is obvious to people from one end of the country to the other. It also means that the American tradition of being a good neighbor and banding together to help those in need is alive and well in an age which is supposed to be characterized by "taking care of number one." The hospice movement is a response to what many perceive as the dual challenges of an over-technologization of medical care and the overt commercialization of health care.

It is only as one begins to read the literature, to speak with persons whose professional interest is death education, and to work with those who teach and counsel about the many forms of and responses to grief that the complexity of the subject becomes more and more apparent. That is why the Hospice Foundation of America has continued to use the teleconference as the focus of a significant effort to provide information and resources to as many people as possible. After all, none of us is immune to grief.

This book reminds us of the central role that loss plays in all of our lives. The chapters included here emphasize the myriad losses and concurrent griefs that individuals with prolonged illness, their families and caregivers experience through the course of the illness experience. The contributors to this book have been selected with care by our editor, Ken Doka, to make sure that many different facets of the subject are discussed by some of the best people in the field. It is our hope that this volume will serve as a resource and a guide for you in your work, your volunteer efforts, your studies, and your personal experiences.

Acknowledgments

First and foremost, I want to acknowledge the authors of these chapters. Each year, as we develop a book for the *Living with Grief* teleconference, our real challenge is to create a book that is a resource in-and-of-itself. To do so means that each author has to accept impossible deadlines. Each year my colleagues are amazed as I repeat that I need their chapters within a comparatively short span. And each year I am astounded that they, in fact, do deliver quality manuscripts within that time frame. I want to thank them all for their understanding and effort.

I wish to thank all those at the Hospice Foundation of America for their continuing support. Its president, Jack D. Gordon, has had the vision to undertake this massive program of education and support. All the past and present staff have each left their mark upon this work.

My own College of New Rochelle, too, has been supportive. My research assistant, Joyce Davidson, has had a major role in editing this work. The book has gained much not only from her editing skills but also from her vision of the project. Rosemary Strobel and Vera Mezzaucella provide ongoing support. My administration and colleagues continue to find their own ways to be supportive.

I also want to acknowledge all those in my personal life who tolerate my work schedules and provide respite. My friends and family, especially Kathy, have continued to give the gift of presence. It has been an interesting year. My son, Michael, has made the transition to adulthood—first major job and his own apartment. I wish him the best. My godson, Keith, is making the transition into adolescence. I wish his mom, Linda, the best.

My coeditor, Joyce Davidson, wishes to acknowledge the support of her family—her husband, Rex, for his support, patience, and encouragement, and Adam and Anne, her two greatest teachers.

Finally, I wish to acknowledge all that I have learned from those whose lives have touched mine. I only hope that these pages reflect a small part of what I have learned from them as I shared their journey through loss.

PART I

Perspectives On Loss: When Illness Is Prolonged

Much about Ed's dying still troubles Margaret. He was in so much pain. Even a loving touch, the change of a dressing, could cause discomfort. Sometimes Ed would respond by lashing out at her. And Margaret, tired from caregiving, would lash back. Ed was tough to look at, too—emaciated by the disease, covered with sores. Even now Margaret sometimes feels physically ill when she thinks of him. The other memories of Ed—the handsome man she married—seem harder to recall. Then there were the decisions. Should she have encouraged that last round of chemotherapy? It did nothing but make him violently ill. The hospice care was wonderful, but did she wait too long before she arranged it?

Margaret's problems are typical of survivors of a death after prolonged illness. Often the grief of survivors of traumatic loss is readily acknowledged. But the death of those who have experienced a more prolonged loss can be minimized by others. Statements such as "It was better for him—he suffered so long," can *disenfranchise* a survivor's grief — that is, not acknowledge that the grief is legitimate and necessary. In addition, the illness experience itself may complicate grief by generating conflicting emotions and creating dilemmas that may cause later pain for the survivors.

Doka, in the opening chapter, explores this further. He identifies three issues: the experience of illness; the extent of suffering; and the

1

difficulty of making medical decisions that can complicate grief for survivors. Doka emphasizes that, for those caring for the dying person, there are opportunities within the illness experience to take actions that can facilitate the grieving process. Hospice personnel, as well as other caregivers, are wise to encourage family and friends to both effectively use this time and draw strength from it.

Davies touches many of the same themes. She notes that as the patient begins to "fade away" there is a constant process of redefinition that needs to occur. This process is essential to re-negotiate relationships and provide effective care; how families handle the transition of fading away affects later grief.

Rando's chapter emphasizes the illness experience as well. One of the myths of prolonged illness is that *anticipatory grief*, the grief that goes on through the illness, mitigates grief after the death. Rando reminds us that the phenomenon of anticipatory grief is much more complex. Her chapter provides two additional critical themes. First, she reminds us that grief is a cognitive process; too often, the cognitive aspects of grief are overlooked in the emphasis on grief's emotional manifestations. Second, she suggests that anticipatory grief meets the criteria of traumatic stress. This critical insight reminds us that survivors of a loved one's prolonged dying process may actually suffer from Posttraumatic Stress Disorder.

In the first chapter, Doka emphasized that the ethical decisions that caregivers make in the course of the illness can affect the grieving process. This important idea is developed further in Price's chapter. He states that "grief can complicate the decisionmaking; less-than-optimal decisionmaking can complicate the grieving." Price emphasizes that caregivers can play a vital role in helping families and patients through a process of sound decisionmaking.

Lamers, a pioneer in the history of hospice, now looks toward its future. Specifically, he considers how new treatments that have prolonged the duration of illness, as well as how new and newly-recognized diseases such as HIV/AIDS and Alzheimer's, challenge the concepts of hospice care. Hospice originally developed as a way to provide humane palliative care to patients in the final stages of cancer. Lamers concludes that these diseases do not challenge the basic concepts of hospice care, but they do challenge present realities of health care and financing.

Lamers' chapter also emphasizes the critical role that hospice care can have in grief adjustment. By controlling symptoms and mitigating suffering, survivors may have less painful memories of the terminal phase, thereby easing grief. In addition, the involvement of family members in the care of the dying person has been effective in easing later grief adjustment (Hamovitch, 1964). Involvement at a comfortable level can give family members the opportunity to see the effects of the disease and to accept the reality of the loss, and give the patient permission to die. Such care also provides opportunity to *finish business*—to say or do something prior to the death and, by those actions, expiate any sense of guilt. Hospice can provide a supportive environment that allows comfortable, family-based care to occur, avoiding the stress that often accompanies grief after prolonged illness.

Finally, Dula's chapter about "Miss Mildred" provides an ethnographic account of the death of an elderly black woman. Dula's chapter reminds how factors such as race and ethnicity can influence the dying process. The chapter also reminds us how important it is to understand the experiences of illness, loss, and grief from the perspective of the person experiencing it. This critical insight emphasizes a theme through this work—listen to each patient's and survivor's individual story.

When Illness Is Prolonged: Implications for Grief

1

Kenneth J. Doka, Ph.D.

Introduction

When Lisa was caring for her mother, who was in the late stages of cancer, the demands of constant caregiving began to take a toll. Even though hospice services provided a health aide for much of the day, Lisa provided care at night. For six weeks, her sleep was interrupted at least three times each evening. Toward the last week of her mother's life, Lisa began to wish that her mother's agony—and hers—would end. Now, after her mother's death, she feels guilty about her feelings.

Tom, too, is troubled by his reaction to his brother's death. When Mark was dying of AIDS Tom visited often, but at the end of Mark's life the physical toll of the disease disturbed Tom. His brother became emaciated by the disease, and his neck and arms were covered with lesions. Tom hated to even touch him; only his deep love and sense of duty compelled him to visit.

"Easy for him, hard for survivors," states the conventional wisdom about sudden loss. Most acknowledge that the suddenness of loss complicates the grief of survivors. There is no time to say goodbye and death is traumatic. Conversely, death after prolonged illness is often considered a blessing or relief. Survivors are seen as having had ample opportunity to grieve the anticipated loss. There is little expectation that grief will be profound, prolonged, or complicated.

Yet the realities of loss are far more complex. While it is clear that sudden losses create complications for survivors (Doka, 1995), prolonged illness can also engender factors that exacerbate grief. Rando (1983) and Sanders (1983) found that both sudden losses and losses after extended illnesses intensified grief. While issues of trauma, preventability, or inability to prepare for the loss certainly trouble survivors of sudden loss, other issues such as disfigurement, suffering, the experience of the illness and the stresses of caregiving, complicate the grief of survivors of the prolonged loss.

The key issue in grief is not to assess what types of losses are easier or harder, but rather to review factors that complicate or facilitate loss in each different circumstance. This chapter attempts to do that in two ways. First, it explores factors that can trouble survivors as they cope with a loss after prolonged illness. Second, it offers suggestions for therapeutic activities that caregivers can use during the illness, as well as at the moment of death and after, to assist grievers, whether those grievers are others or oneself. Prior to this it is critical to understand the process of a prolonged life-threatening illness. For often, issues at any point in the illness may have subsequent effects on grief.

The Process of Life-Threatening Illness

A prolonged life-threatening illness is best viewed as a series of phases (Doka, 1993). The first phase may be described as the *prediagnostic phase.* This is the period of time between when a person first suspects a problem and when that person seeks medical advice. Few people immediately run to a physician at the first sign of a symptom. It is important to explore this phase for a number of reasons.

This process can reveal much about the ways that a person will cope with life-threatening illness. John, a 56-year-old man, was experiencing frequent and severe headaches. For a long time he simply tried to ignore the problem and self-medicated. As the headaches continued, he began to become anxious, eventually seeking medical help. He never shared his fears, or even the fact that he was undergoing testing, with his wife until he needed to be hospitalized when diagnosed with a brain tumor. Throughout his illness, John tended to exhibit much of the same behavior; he continued to deny the seriousness of the illness, delayed treatments and coped alone.

Decisions made at this time by either the ill individual or the caretakers can reverberate for survivors throughout the grieving period. When John eventually died, his wife was tormented by her belief that she should have recognized his discomfort and made him seek medical help earlier.

The second phase, the *acute phase*, is characterized as the crisis of diagnosis. Many families describe this crisis as a major one, second only to the death itself. This phase actually may extend over a period of weeks as the individual undergoes a series of medical tests that gradually narrow the diagnosis. In this process, both patients and their families may begin to experience *anticipatory grief.* Such grief is not only an anticipation of a future possible loss, but also a reaction to the losses being experienced, such as losses of health, mobility, and future plans.

In a prolonged illness, the *chronic phase* tends to have significant implications for the subsequent grief of survivors. This phase is the period when the goal of medical treatment is still to seek a cure or extend life. It can be a very difficult time both for patients and their families. Friends and family who were so present during the crisis around the diagnosis tend to return to their own lives. The patient needs to cope with the symptoms of the disease, the side effects of treatment, and, in many cases, the ongoing demands of life, such as home, family, and work. If the illness creates significant disability, family members may be called upon to assume significant caregiving tasks in addition to their ongoing roles. They must cope together with the stress, feelings and anxieties that the illness generates. Often their own plans are contingent on the patient's illness.

The nature of stresses in the chronic phase will be influenced strongly by the pattern of the illness. Some illnesses, such as multiple sclerosis, have a pattern characterized by descents that then stabilize for a while at a new level of disability. Other diseases—leukemia and AIDS, for example—have patterns of remission and relapse. Still others, including degenerative diseases like muscular dystrophy or some forms of cancer, show long, slow declines in health and functioning.

Each of these patterns creates unique issues for survivors. For example, family members coping with the stress of caring for a patient during a period of slow decline may experience a strong sense of relief along with the grief. These natural feelings of relief at the death may generate significant guilt.

In some cases, patients may temporarily enter a *recovery phase*, where they and their families believe that the illness has been cured or controlled. John and his physician hoped that the surgery had fully removed the brain tumor. John's functioning returned to normal levels, and for two years he believed the illness was behind him. Even in this period, John reported three responses typical in recovery. First, he experienced a new sense of appreciation for life and began to reorder his priorities. Second, he realized that the illness had changed his life in a number of ways, some of which were not favorable. Given his insurance risk, he felt locked in his job, and he also believed that he was unlikely to be promoted beyond his present level. Finally, even though John believed he was cured, he constantly struggled with anxiety. Each new headache or pain brought intense fear of cancer.

In the *terminal phase* the goal of treatment shifts from cure or control to comfort. Here, the patient and family begin to prepare for eventual death. Both may need to make or review decisions on such questions as whether or not to enter a hospice program, whether or when to terminate certain treatments or withdraw life support and who should be empowered to make decisions should the patient no longer be able. The decisions made about these issues may reverberate throughout the grieving process.

Living with Grief After Prolonged Ilness

Whenever one experiences loss, certain reactions are common. Grief affects at all levels—physically, emotionally, cognitively, behaviorally, and spiritually. Physically, bereaved persons may experience a variety of reactions including physical aches and pains, nausea, or insomnia. Tiredness is typical too, as the body compensates for long periods of operating under stress.

Emotional reactions are also common. Any feelings—anger, jealousy, anxiety and sadness, to name just a few — may be evident. Two deserve special mention. Sometimes survivors may experience a sense of relief or emancipation. The burdens of caregiving have ceased, as has the deceased's suffering. As mentioned earlier, these feelings may generate guilt. Survivors may also feel guilty about decisions made during the course of the illness. They may experience 'moral' guilt, believing the illness and suffering of the deceased were a punishment for their transgressions. They may experience 'role' guilt as well, regretting that they were not a better spouse or child. This type of guilt can be very evident after a prolonged illness where the strains of constant caregiving exacerbate tensions or provoke anger and resentment toward the ill person.

Cognitive reactions can include depersonalization, confusion and disorientation. Survivors may actually behave differently, or find it difficult to concentrate. Some survivors may seek reminders of the deceased; others may avoid such reminders. Some may find it difficult to engage in activity; others may seek diversion in constant activity.

Spiritually, grief has many manifestations. Some persons may search for meaning in the loss. Some may return to their spiritual roots, while others may question their spiritual and religious beliefs. Even the great Christian apologist, C.S. Lewis, reacted with a strong sense of spiritual alienation when his wife died of cancer. "Where is God when you need him? . . . A door slammed in your face. . . ." (Lewis, 1961, p. 4). Later he could realize it was his own frantic need that slammed that door.

All of these reactions are common to any grief. And the experience of grief, as in any loss, is highly individual, dependent on the nature of the relationship and the personality and coping styles of the bereaved, as well as the availability of informal and formal support. Yet when loss follows a prolonged illness, several factors can complicate the grief of survivors.

1. The Experience of Illness

First, there is the meaning of the disease. As Sontag (1978) reminds us, diseases are steeped in meaning. They are not simply perceived as biological processes but carry psychological and social implications as well that vary among individuals. For some individuals a diagnosis of AIDS simply is viewed as a tragic viral infection. Others may view it as a shameful stigma or a punishment from God. The degree to which a disease is defined with negative meanings by survivors or others in their community may affect the willingness or ability of survivors to seek and obtain support. For example, if survivors define AIDS as shameful, they may be reluctant to share their loss with others, effectively disenfranchising their grief. If survivors define it as a punishment from God, their spirituality may give scant comfort; in fact, their spiritual struggle is likely to complicate their grief.

Not only the meaning but the nature of the disease may affect the grief of survivors. Each disease has its own unique symptoms, treatment and side effects, and pattern, and each will affect the grief of survivors differently.

Two critical symptoms that have significant effects on grief are disfigurement and mental disorientation and/or personality change. Disfigurement, especially facial, can create strong ambivalent feelings in family members. While they love the person, they may be physically repulsed by them. Such feelings later can generate strong feelings of guilt. One mother, whose adult son died of AIDS, succinctly described these reactions:

> In the end he had wasted away to a skeleton. There were red lesions. He was always so handsome. Now I couldn't even bear to look at him, to touch him. One day after I bathed him, I actually had to vomit. I hope he didn't know. I am so ashamed.

Mental deterioration and personality change are not uncommon in prolonged illness. In some illnesses, like Alzheimer's, it is the essence of the disease. In others, such as AIDS or some forms of cancer, it can occur either as a direct result of the disease process or as a side effect of treatment. In some other cases, patients, given the psychological stress of a prolonged illness as well as facing death, may cope in ways uncharacteristic of prior behavior.

Such changes can have many effects on the grieving process. In and of themselves they create an additional loss that survivors must experience. They also can generate strong feelings of ambivalence, anger and resentment. Survivors are now caring for a very different person from the one they once knew. For example, one wife recounted her experiences with her husband as he died of a brain tumor:

> In the end, he became so different—he was so angry and hateful. I kept saying 'This is not the man I married,' but I wondered where all this hate came from. Was it the tumor, the medication, or was this always a part of him that stayed hidden? Sometimes even now I think, 'How much of my marriage was real?'

This case illustrates another aspect of mental deterioration and/or personality change. Her husband's angry outbursts caused conflict between them in the terminal phase, leaving her, at his death, with much guilt and considerable unfinished business.

2. The Extent of a Patient's Suffering

The perception of how much a patient suffered in a prolonged illness can influence grief in four ways. First, it can contribute to feelings of helplessness among family members. Second, suffering can generate ambivalence about the patient's continued living. The patient's intimate network may truly want that person to live, but they may also want the patient's suffering, as well as their vicarious suffering, to end. Later, survivors may feel guilty about wishing for the patient's death. They also may feel guilty about their grief, thinking it selfish to grieve a merciful death.

Third, the perception that the patient suffered greatly may diminish the social support available to immediate survivors. Comments such as "It's better he's dead, he suffered so much," serve to effectively disenfranchise grief.

Finally, the question of suffering can deeply trouble survivors' spirituality. They may find themselves angry with God or find their own spirituality inadequate in providing a framework to understand the suffering. This can rob survivors of the strength their spirituality previously provided.

3. The Issue of Medical Decisions

Throughout the course of a prolonged illness, patients and their families have to make more decisions now than they did in the past. While years ago there may have been few options in treatment, now individuals may need to decide among a variety of options. Should one treat a problem such as cancer surgically, using chemotherapy or radiation therapy? Even within therapies there are options. How radical should the surgery be? What course of chemotherapy should one select? When should care become palliative, not curative? Should one attempt to be on an experimental protocol? In addition to conventional options, patients and their families may have to negotiate a host of nonconventional therapies—some complementary, like imaging, and some true alternative therapies that exist outside of and often preclude conventional medical treatment.

Technology, too, is complex and has created ethical issues. In many ways, struggles with issues of euthanasia and abortion derive from a similar difficulty in defining the beginnings and ends of life. Living wills and advance directives may help clarify a patient's wishes and assist families with discussions over these issues, but there still are considerable areas of gray. When should treatment stop? What treatments should be terminated? Who is responsible for ultimately making these decisions?

Beyond the complexities of treatment and technology, there is another significant factor that has contributed to the patient's and family's increased role in medical decisionmaking. Due to concerns about liability, as well as increased attention to a patient's autonomy and rights, many physicians are reluctant to offer strong advice and direction. Many physicians instead see their role as presenting an array of options for patients to decide. While this enhances patient autonomy, patients and their families may feel overwhelmed and unprepared as they make medical decisions.

After the patient dies, family members may be inclined to second guess those decisions. This can complicate the grieving process, generating further anger or guilt. In some cases it may even exacerbate conflicts between family members if they blame one another for choices made. Such conflicts may divert energy from grief and limit social support.

Interventions for Grief in Prolonged Illness

While there may be factors that complicate grief when illness is prolonged, the extended time of the illness does offer opportunity for activities and interventions during the illness, and at the time of death, that can mitigate grief. And, as with all losses, there also are activities and interventions helpful to survivors after the loss.

Throughout the illness, caregivers can assist families in acknowledging the many responses they may be having. Especially in the terminal phase, family members may be troubled by feelings of ambivalence—hoping that the individual's struggle, and their own, is nearing an end. If the dying person begins to withdraw, family members may feel confused, hurt, and rejected. They may be physically exhausted. Guilt, anger, and sadness are common. They may feel awkward, unsure of what to say or do. Helping families to acknowledge and address these feelings prior to loss may help later grief.

Two actions that can be extremely helpful in this period are remembrance and ritual. Reminiscence can be powerful both for the dying person and for friends and family. For the dying person, reminiscence reinforces the sense that one's life had meaning and purpose. For family and friends, it provides an opportunity to share memories and to finish business. In some cases, it may allow a moment to accept or offer forgiveness or even simply to clarify feelings. Later, family and friends can take comfort in these moments, feeling that they were able to share love.

Rituals, too, can be significant ways to finish business and to say goodbye. For example, the Roman Catholic Ritual of Anointing the Sick can give families and patients a sense of religious comfort. But rituals need not be overtly religious. In one family, a dying father simply hugged each of his children, giving each one a special gift. And rituals, because they involve activity, can also reaffirm a sense of control in an otherwise uncontrollable situation.

Other activities can serve a similar purpose. One of the great values of hospice care is that it keeps the family directly involved in the care of the dying person. To the extent that families are both able and comfortable, this process can mitigate later grief. Family members may be more aware of the suffering, and thus are more prepared to accept the death. In addition, ongoing involvement provides opportunities for non-verbal acts or feelings. After the death, survivors can remember, and be encouraged to recount, the many ways they demonstrated care. However, a key issue is respecting limits of comfort. Survivors may be troubled at the physical deterioration of the dying person and disturbed by their own feelings of repulsion and perhaps withdrawal.

Many of these activities can be encouraged with comatose patients as well. Often simple acts such as stroking the person or taking part in routine physical care can assuage feelings of uselessness. This period, too, can be a meaningful opportunity for family members to take leave and finish remaining business, saying things to the comatose person that might have otherwise caused discomfort.

The time of death provides other important moments. Survivors need not be rushed out of the room. They may wish to exercise the option to spend time with the deceased, perhaps to say a few closing words or perform a special act such as dressing or washing the body.

After the death, survivors need to struggle with their loss. Like other survivors, they will experience the roller coaster of grief reactions, including physical, emotional, cognitive, behavioral, and spiritual manifestations. Often, it is helpful to review the illness experience with survivors, beginning with their experience even before the diagnosis. This will provide an opportunity to assess any issues from the illness that may affect the grieving process.

While survivors of a loss through prolonged illness struggle with many issues common to anyone experiencing grief, one unique issue is the need for survivors to recapture the image of the person prior to his or her illness. When an illness is prolonged and the dying person slowly fades away, images of the person at the time of the illness can overwhelm earlier, more positive and vibrant images. Many of the interventions mentioned before, such as reminiscence and ritual, as well as reviewing photographs, can reaffirm those previous images. Funeral homes, too, can play a significant role when they prepare the deceased to look more as he or she was prior to the ravages of the illness.

Conclusion

While these actions may help mitigate grief, it is critical to affirm that survivors of someone who has died because of a prolonged illness will still experience grief. That grief must be coped with, in each survivor's own individual style.

One of the myths that often troubles survivors of a death after prolonged illness is the belief that the death itself was a mercy and that they had ample time to adjust to the loss. As this chapter has indicated, each type of death creates its own unique issues for survivors. The fact that a prolonged illness preceded a death does not necessarily mean that the death was either expected or welcomed. Many survivors can have a profound sense that the death was not expected at the time it occurred (Doka, 1984). And even if there are feelings of relief, these feelings are simply part of the mix of feelings that make up the process of grieving.

A key issue with survivors when loss is prolonged is not to disenfranchise their grief. Disenfranchised grief occurs when a loss is negated and the survivors' right to grieve is unsupported (Doka, 1989). The antidote to disenfranchised grief lies in the simple acknowledgment that every circumstance of loss, including loss after prolonged illness, creates its own unique grief.

Fading Away During Terminal Illness: Implications for Bereavement in Family Members

2

Betty Davies, R.N., Ph.D.

The study of grief and bereavement over the past 20 years has resulted in an examination of many factors that influence bereavement following the death of a family member. Questions about how the cause of death, specifically sudden death or death following chronic illness, impacts upon bereavement outcome have been widely debated, with general agreement that sudden death results in less favorable bereavement outcome (Sanders, 1982–83). The concept of *anticipatory grief* is commonly used to explain the difference. When individuals have an opportunity to prepare emotionally for the impending death, serious medical, psychological, and social risks are diminished. This work has been extended in recent years to examine other variables that might affect bereavement outcome following prolonged death, specifically from cancer. Effects of hospice care have received wide attention (Barzelai, 1981; Lack and Buckingham, 1978), with focus on several factors, including location of care, duration of illness, length of hospice care prior to death, and satisfaction with care of the loved one (Steele, 1990; Yancy, Greger and Coburn, 1990). In addition to these variables, which focus primarily on the circumstances surrounding the death, other factors must be considered. Families' perceptions of their own experience with a terminally-ill member is an important factor that impacts upon bereavement of surviving family members.

The entire family unit is affected when one of its members is terminally ill. Anything that affects the family system affects the individual members, just as the individual members affect the family as a whole. Therefore, it is critical to understand how the family's experience during the terminal phase of illness impacts upon the surviving members following the patient's death. Findings from a program of research that focused on the experience of families having a member with advanced cancer generated a model that conceptualized families' experiences as a transition—a transition which families themselves labeled as "fading away." This paper will begin with a brief summary of this transition. For a more in-depth description, the reader is referred to Davies, Chekryn-Reimer, Brown and Martens (1995). The remainder of the paper will discuss the centrality of one aspect of the transition, redefining, and its impact upon the bereavement of spouses and teenage and young adult children following the death of a loved one from cancer.

The Transition of Fading Away

Families with a member who has terminal cancer are in transition: the transition from living with to dying from cancer. The transition begins when family members recognize the decline in the patient's physical condition and realize he or she will not recover. The patient's condition deteriorates to the point where the inevitable can no longer be denied. The patient may lose weight, become weaker, less mobile or less mentally alert. As one woman said, "I get weaker and weaker . . . I can't eat as much . . . I'm fading. I know I'm fading." The physiological changes limit or alter how family members experience the one who is dying, and how the dying person experiences life. However, it is important to note that fading away encompasses more than a physical fading away. It also includes the process of change as it affects all family members, including the patient, as well as the family unit as a whole.

The transition of fading away incorporates seven components that are interrelated: *redefining, burdening, contending with change, struggling with paradox, searching for meaning, living day-to-day,* and *preparing for death.* They can be likened to the threads of a tapestry in the making. Threads of varying colors and textures are interwoven to create the evolving scene. Like threads of different colors, each phase recurs and overlaps with others, not necessarily in the same sequence each time it reappears.

The transition must begin with the patient's redefinition of self and other family members' redefinition of the patient. Redefining continues throughout the fading away with no clear ending and is the basis for the other components of the fading-away process. The patient confronts the possibility of being a burden, and family members grapple with being burdened by the extra responsibilities inherent in caring for a dying member. The family struggles with several paradoxes that derive from the central paradox of the patient living with cancer while dying from cancer. All family members face major changes in their lives and search for meaning to find some way of coming to terms with the experience. As the end draws near, the patient and other family members live day-to-day and prepare for the impending death.

Centrality of Redefining

The realization that a loved one is dying results in a major change for the entire family. Family members adjust not only outwardly but also inwardly, where they keep connections to the people and places that support definitions of self. Redefining involves a shift in terms of what used to be and what is now and leads to an adjustment in how individuals view themselves and each other, as well as how they define the family unit. The family accommodates to changes in the patient's status through redefining and copes with the losses and gains incurred.

Family members' readiness to redefine the patient as different is critical to their ability to accommodate changes imposed by the illness. They need to relinquish former views of themselves and others in the family and adjust their behavior and patterns of living. The patient's redefinition of self is the central factor in this process. When patients succeed at redefining themselves, they ease the process for others in the family. When patients are able to acknowledge that they are dying and change their behavior accordingly, family members are also able to deal more effectively with the transition. If any member of a family remains unwilling to redefine the patient, re-definition for the other family members is impeded and results in resistance to changes in patterns of living, creating tension as family members try to evade the effects of the illness and act as if little has changed. Although family members may redefine at different times, personal and interpersonal frustration results if disjunction persists.

Redefining for Patients

Redefining for patients means letting go of their view of who they used to be and developing a new view of themselves and others. Patients alter their identity over time. As their capacities become more limited, their identity narrows. They relinquish certain aspects of themselves: "I can't do the physical work anymore . . . I had to accept that, with the seizures I was having, I couldn't go back to that role [supervisor in a gas plant]." Patients often maintain their normal patterns for as long as possible, and then implement feasible alternatives. They make the adjustments that their declining state demands. They seem to accept their situation and make the best of it, though it may be difficult to accept the limitations imposed by the disease. They speak about their new selves with sadness and a sense of loss: "It's not easy to give up so many things I love to do, but I have learned that you have to let go—and let other people do those things I used to do." In redefining themselves, they differentiate those aspects which remain intact and those which have changed: "It's hard to recognize me when I look in the mirror, but inside, I'm still me." When patients redefine themselves as dying, but still recognize their accomplishments and retain their sense of self (either through new ways of thinking or by exploring spiritual issues), they then achieve reasonable contentment. They convey this contentment to other family members, making it easier for spouses and children to redefine the patient and themselves.

When patients recognize changes in themselves, but do not allow these changes to alter their regular patterns, they redefine themselves to a lesser degree. Their definitions of self do not fit with the changing reality. Instead, they try to continue as if everything were the same, but become irritated by their inability to do so and are persistently frustrated and angry. Mr. P., for example, recognized his physical weakness, but continued his workaholic pattern up until he died: ". . . I stuccoed part of the garage with a finished pattern. I did that Friday. It was all I could do . . . It just about killed me. I couldn't hold up anything, I was so weak . . ." Mrs. P. was extremely frustrated with her husband's behavior: "He doesn't want to see how sick he is—he goes on as if nothing is wrong. He was too weak to be out in the garage . . . what can I do? He won't listen! I just let him be . . ." When patients have difficulty redefining themselves, their discontent distances them from others, and patients often feel abandoned, isolated and unsupported.

Redefining for Spouses

Redefining by spouses also plays a critical role in how they manage during the terminal phase of the patient's illness. When spouses redefine the patient, they acknowledge the physical changes, but take these in stride. They remain aware of the changing nature of the patient's condition and interpret the subtle changes as taking away hope for recovery: "As I see him waste away, fall asleep at a moment's notice, unable to move around, I know that hope is fading." Spouses often focus on understanding the ill person's perspective on the physical changes: "I think of how difficult it would be to be in a body that has changed so much." Spouses' redefining physical aspects of the patient occurs independently of the patient's perceptions of his or her own bodily changes. However, a central feature of spouses' redefining has to do with their relationship with the patient. The ease with which they redefine the relationship relates to the patient's success at redefining him or herself.

When patients and spouses redefine, they devote time to redefining their relationship. Together, they adjust their plans accordingly and reorganize their priorities to make the most of the shared time they have left. One woman explained, "We know our time is limited, so I went to working only part time. We want to spend more time together. Instead of going out like we used to, we stay home and quietly watch TV or read together, just enjoying each other's company." When patients redefine themselves appropriately and spouses redefine their priorities, spouses feel more content and are satisfied with their support of the patient. Some spouses feel closer to the patient. They describe their relationship with the patient as reciprocal, not one-sided. They believe their relationship grows.

When patients do not redefine, spouses cannot redefine the relationship, and the relationship suffers. Spouses try to continue as normal, becoming exhausted trying to maintain daily life as if nothing has changed. Mr. P. maintained his workaholic patterns, though he acknowledged that he had some physical limitations. This served to push others away and made life very hard for his wife. She saw the physical changes in him and understood his need to work, but because he stubbornly clung to his former image of himself, she found the relationship trying. When there is little redefinition on the part of the patient, spouses avoid situations that force the patient to confront the need for change.

When redefining is limited, struggling with paradox and contending with change are made more difficult. Moreover, when there is less redefining, there is less need to search for meaning, since seemingly nothing has really changed. Spouses in such situations are exhausted—from caring for a patient who doesn't want to admit the need to be cared for, from avoiding any discussion or action that would remind the patient of his or her deteriorating condition, and from feeling that their efforts are unappreciated by their partners. They do not experience any sense of personal growth from the experience; they simply endure it and wait for it to end.

Redefining for Children

Aspects of redefining by teenage and young adult children have more to do with their developmental stages than with the patient's redefinition of self. However, changes in the patient's physical condition impact profoundly on the adult children. The drastic changes require a major shift in perception of their parent from someone strong and in control to someone who is now the opposite: "I always thought of him as, not invulnerable, but a very strong individual . . . [his illness] has made me step back and take another look at him." Many come face-to-face with mortality for the first time. Realizing that their parent faces death, young adults redefine themselves as vulnerable—they realize that they too will die. Part of redefining for children means facing the future without the parent.

Adult children are faced with numerous responsibilities when a parent is dying, often assuming many caregiving, financial, and emotional responsibilities for their ill parent as well as for their healthy parent. The demands are great at a time when these young adults are developing their own intimate relationships, establishing careers, or meeting the needs of their own spouses and children. They are pulled in many directions and are exhausted. While spouses, especially those whose partners have redefined themselves, are able to see some good come of their experience, children seldom see any good in the experience. They contend with changes in every aspect of their lives.

In contrast to the successful redefinition of their parent, some adult children may continue as if nothing has changed and try to recapture an idealized past. These individuals devote all their attention to their relationship with the patient and to creating a "perfect" family, which causes tension and conflict. They may spend time trying to replace what they believe has been neglected. In doing so, they neglect their own spouses and children. Bob S., for example, regretted that he did not share what he considered a close relationship with his mother. During her youth, economic depression had forced her to quit school in the eighth grade. Bob, who was pursuing doctoral studies, felt that his uneducated mother had never understood his academic world. During the last months of her life, Bob traveled 600 miles every two weeks to visit her in an attempt to capture the closeness he yearned for. Though she appreciated her son's visits, Mrs. S. found them trying, since her son talked constantly and made little progress toward his goal of making his mother understand him.

When the children are teenagers, redefining is also jeopardized. A developmental challenge for teenagers is balancing their desire for independence with the security afforded by childhood. The serious illness and death of a parent greatly interfere with how teenagers face this challenge. Teenagers demonstrate a reluctance to redefine their parent, despite obvious deterioration in their parent's physical condition. They hold on to the old view of their parent as much as they can by trying not to think about the fact that he or she is seriously ill: "I don't see cancer when I see my mom. I just see her as my mom . . . I never think about it. I try not to think about it." Not thinking about it helps teenagers quell their fears about living in the future without their parent. By maintaining their old view of their ill parent, teenagers do not need to redefine themselves as facing the future without their parents, and hence need not face their fears of abandonment.

Moreover, having a seriously ill parent disrupts the teenager's normal process of breaking away from family, shatters their security, and draws them back into the family. They feel burdened by the extra responsibilities and resent the changes imposed by the illness. Teenagers lack the same ability as older children to look into the future and see the inevitability of death. Hence, they do not feel the need to make the most of the time they have left with their parent. Their search for meaning usually does not demonstrate much reflective thinking about the illness in relation to their own values and attitudes. Their response to a dying parent is characterized primarily by *shielding*—by protecting themselves from a reality for which they are not ready. Patients' own sense of relative contentment can offer strength to frightened teens, but cannot fully overcome the teenagers' tendency to shield themselves from such bad news. Parents who are able to redefine are more likely to create an environment in which teenagers can face the reality of impending death.

Redefining/Family Functioning

How patients and family members manage the transition of fading away is related to individuals' ways of being in the world. However, individuals' responses occur not in isolation, but within the context of their families. Families have their own styles of interacting. How families interact contributes to their success or difficulty with the transition, based on the following eight dimensions: *integrating the past, dealing with feelings, solving problems, utilizing resources, considering others, portraying family identity, fulfilling roles,* and *tolerating differences.* These dimensions occur along a continuum; family interactions tend to vary along the continuum rather than being good or bad, positive or negative.

Of particular importance is the fact that the dimensions of family functioning are related to the way in which individual members redefine their current situation. In some families, painful past experiences are incorporated into the ongoing life of the family as events from which members learned valuable lessons. Some families openly express a wide range of feelings, including happiness and sadness, uncertainty or dread. They acknowledge and share their vulnerabilities and fears, their hopes and dreams. They describe their ambivalence about the patient's continuous decline and their responses. They identify problems as they arise, discuss possible strategies and agree upon a solution. Patients in families characterized in these ways are more likely to redefine their situations realistically and make the necessary adaptations.

On the other hand, when patients redefine themselves, their attitude helps create a more comfortable atmosphere because energy can be directed toward enjoying each other's company and doing what needs to be done, instead of trying to maintain a false sense of normalcy. Moreover, such an atmosphere extends a welcome to individuals outside the immediate family, whose presence increases the likelihood of ongoing social support throughout the terminal phase and into bereavement.

In contrast, when families cling to past traumatic experiences and continue to dwell on painful feelings associated with past events, they are more insistent on carrying on as if everything were unchanged in the current situation. Members often direct their energy to recreating the past so that they have happy memories (recall Bob's attempt at reconciling his relationship with his mother). The mode of interaction in these families is to not acknowledge feelings or uncertainties. Members ignore problems or assign blame for them and do not achieve resolution. They appear reluctant to seek or accept any help. The pattern is for individuals to focus on their own emotional needs with little regard for others, and redefining in these families is less likely to occur. As a result, there is less opportunity for family members to enhance their relationships with the patient or with each other, to find meaning in the situation, or to prepare for the impending death and for life following the death.

Redefining: Implications for Caregiving and Bereavement

It is often said that family member's involvement in caregiving prior to a loved one's death facilitates their grieving following the patient's death. All spouses in this study provided care for their dying partners. However, the experiences of spouses varied considerably, depending on the degree to which the patient redefined his or her situation, which in turn influenced the degree to which they were aware of being a burden to their loved ones. When patients redefine themselves, they are sensitive to being a burden and try their best to alleviate the burden for their loved ones. The result is a better caregiving experience for family members, which lays the groundwork for a better experience during bereavement as well.

Patients feel they are a burden to their loved ones because of the extra work that their situation demands. They are also concerned that these demands prevent family members from carrying on with their lives. However, patients vary in the degree to which they believe themselves to be a burden. Their perception of burden is related to the degree to which they have not constructively redefined themselves. When patients do redefine themselves, they are better able to direct their limited and depleting energy toward others, are more likely to see that their illness creates a burden, and are more concerned about the resultant strain on their loved ones.

They attempt to alleviate the burden in several ways. They try not to complain: "There's no way I would want to put any greater burden on them . . . by moaning and groaning and crying about the situation." In another approach, they utilize the skills and strengths they still have to do as much as possible to help. Mrs. J., for example, wanted to relieve the burden of extra housekeeping responsibilities on her husband and daughter. She managed to sweep the floor by slowly maneuvering her wheelchair around the kitchen, though she could not bend over to use the dustpan: "Even this little bit helps save them—they have so much to do now and I like to help as much as I can." Mrs. J.'s daughter commented about her mother's sweeping the floor: "Mom does all she can. Seeing her try so hard makes me want to try harder too." Perceiving that the patient acknowledges and appreciates their efforts, family members feel satisfied with their care and are motivated to continue to give that care generously. After the patient's death, they will find comfort in knowing they provided the best possible care and that their efforts were appreciated.

Patients also help by altering the nature of their contributions from direct action to instruction. When one patient could no longer change the oil in his daughter's car, he asked to be taken outside in his wheelchair and instructed his daughter, step-by-step, so that she could change the oil herself. Both father and daughter were very proud of her newly-acquired skill. After her father's death, the daughter will continue to feel proud of her new skill and will be grateful for her father's assistance in preparing her to function independently.

Recognizing the extra strain on their loved ones, patients encourage family members to continue with "normal" activities, such as socializing, as much as they can. Mrs. J. told her husband, "It's Thursday night—it's your club night. I want you to go and have a good time; take a break from all that you have been doing around the house; I will be fine. If I need anything, S. [neighbor] is just next door, and I can call her." Mr. J. responded: "It's a life-saver—a way just to keep in touch with the rest of the world because my world is now looking after my wife. I don't mind doing it either—but it is good to get out and see the fellows down at the club. It recharges my batteries." Mr. J. was re-energized and better able to continue caring for his dying wife. After her death, he will suffer the fatigue that normally accompanies grief, but his reserve stocks will not be as depleted as they would have been had he not had his regular nights at the club. Moreover, the camaraderie with his "fellows" not only supports him during the terminal phase of his wife's illness, but will likely continue after her death.

When patients do not redefine themselves, they use their limited energy to maintain their former view of themselves, often at the expense of the spouse-caregiver, and the burden on family members is increased. Patients do not even recognize the burden they place on family members. Mr. P. said, "I can't do anything. It's a burden on my wife, but I do a bit yet . . . sure, there's some extra work for her, but I don't think it's all that much." When patients minimize or deny the strain on family members they underestimate the demands they place on others. Rather than trying to alleviate burden, they add to it. Unable to redefine himself, Mr. P. struggled to carry on with his daily routines as if nothing had changed. He assumed that his wife would simply do what he could no longer do, without recognizing the extra responsibilities his care involved. He had a habit of adopting stray dogs. Now, unable to feed or walk his dogs, Mr. P. assumed that his wife would care for them. Moreover, he became angry when he saw her with the dogs, a bitter reminder of his growing inability. Discussing the situation with her husband was out of the question, so Mrs. P. walked the dogs early in the morning and late at night when her husband was asleep, during times when she herself required much-needed rest. Mrs. P. felt unappreciated and overworked, but more importantly, she resented her husband's stubbornness and could not tell him for fear of making him even more irritable.

Mrs. P. felt that her husband took her efforts for granted, without recognizing the strain she experienced. She was frustrated, discouraged, and rejected. She resigned herself to continuing her care as best she could, but was exhausted and simply "endured" the time until her husband died. Consequently, after his death, Mrs. P. will not have memories of a satisfying relationship with her husband. When individuals feel ambivalent toward the deceased, or harbor feelings of unresolved anger or resentment, they face additional challenges in bereavement. Mrs. P. will likely be dissatisfied with the care she was able to give, since it never seemed adequate to her husband. During bereavement, her frustration may continue, perhaps compounded by regretting that she could not provide better care, or by anger from knowing that the situation would have been better had her husband been more realistic. Her feelings of rejection may also impact negatively on her self-esteem and her confidence in being able to manage her grief. She will be physically and emotionally exhausted by the time her husband dies.

All family members who care for a dying loved one struggle with chronic fatigue. However, when redefining occurs, patients encourage family members to attend to their own needs. Patients' appreciation of their caregivers' needs for rest and self-care contributes to the caregivers' well-being. Mr. Q. described how he considered his wife's needs: "She wakes up every two hours to check on me, so I wait until then to ask her for more pain reliever. She needs her sleep—it's hard work looking after me." His wife, appreciative of her husband's efforts, commented: "He does everything he can to make it easier for me, and I do everything I can for him. It makes it so much easier to care for him—even getting up every two hours."

Those who have not received such appreciation from patients are physically exhausted by the time the death occurs. Mrs. L. provides an example. Mr. L. called his wife persistently for help with no regard for her need to rest: "She rests when I am sleeping, I think. I have a lot of pain, and she brings me the medicine when I need it." Mrs. L. was worn out and barely able to keep going. "I do what I can for him, but I can't do any more—he wouldn't notice anyway." Moreover, Mrs. L. had severe varicose veins and arthritis for which she simply did not have the time or energy to arrange a visit to her doctor. Cumulative fatigue and lack of attention to personal health contribute to stress and lower resistance to illness during bereavement.

Implications for Practitioners

When working with the bereaved, practitioners will find it helpful to review the individual's experience during the terminal phase of the loved one's illness. If redefining was limited, practitioners need to be aware that the surviving family members may be suffering from long-standing exhaustion, both physical and emotional, in addition to the normal fatigue that accompanies grief. Family members may be in a poor state of health from having put their own needs on hold for the sake of the patient. Attention to physical status may be required now. Practitioners can help family members appreciate the need to take care of their own needs.

Family members may harbor regrets about the extent or quality of care they were able to provide their loved one and may resent the patient's lack of acknowledgment or appreciation for the care family members did offer. Practitioners should review with family members the extent of the care they provided, and acknowledge the burden they bore. For children, acknowledge their efforts in adjusting their usual routines to accommodate the extra demands when their ill parent was dying. Acknowledge that their visits, keeping in touch, staying available by phone or managing financial documents, all represent the work of caring and should not be underestimated.

Family members may feel guilty for wishing the patient would die so the struggle would end. Do not minimize their pain, but reassure them that struggling with the paradox of simultaneously living with and dying from cancer is a normal manifestation of coping with terminal illness. Explain that the conflicting feelings of wanting to help while resenting the extra demands are normal.

By the time the parent dies, family members may have limited support to assist them during their bereavement. If the decreased social support stems from their having had to withdraw from normal social activities while they were caring for the dying patient, encourage them to begin to reinvest in previous social activities. Bereaved spouses may have limited support from their adult children. Adult children may have been burdened with heavy responsibilities during the illness and now are eager to devote more time to their own spouses and children or to their own careers, which they put on hold during their parent's illness. Encourage those children to reassure the surviving parent that they have not abandoned them and will not neglect them. Reassure them that getting on with their own lives is necessary for the sake of their careers or family and acknowledge the ongoing difficulty of having to balance their own lives with caring for a bereaved parent.

Adult children are often depleted and exhausted. Despite their contributions, they may feel guilty over not having done enough for their ill parent, for resenting their extra responsibilities, or for ignoring their own spouses and children while attending to their parents' needs. During bereavement, they must deal with such feelings while continuing with families and careers that demand considerable attention. There is little free time for young adults to reflect and to allow themselves time to grieve adequately. Practitioners may explain that serious illness and death often force people to a far-reaching examination of their values, beliefs, and goals. Suggest approaches for ongoing personal reflection, such as journal writing.

Parents of grieving teenagers face additional challenges. Practitioners must explain to parents that teenagers were not fully prepared for death because of the way in which they shielded themselves from this reality. Teenagers grieving a parent's death benefit from programs that help them achieve healthy completion of developmental tasks. They benefit from an atmosphere of sharing ideas, information and feelings regarding death and loss issues.

Practitioners working with grieving individuals following a prolonged illness also need to explore the family's way of functioning as a way to assist the grieving family members. Part of understanding the family includes having family members tell their stories. In some families, stories will tend to be repeated, and the feelings associated with them will resurface. Some families will spend considerable time reviewing painful aspects of their past. This may be helpful to release pent-up emotions, but it may also be a style of functioning that interferes with redefining the current situation. Similarly, because of their history, some families find they cannot pull together to cope with the stress of terminal illness or bereavement.

In families where there is consensus about problems and issues, open and direct communication, and flexibility toward change, practitioners can approach the family as a cohesive unit, confident that grieving family members have adequate support. In other families— where communication is relatively indirect, where there is little agreement about the nature of significant issues, where roles are rigidly entrenched, and there is little tolerance for differences of opinion— practitioners must be more concerned about the course of bereavement in family members. In all types of families, practitioners need to listen to the stories that members tell.

The ways in which families function remain relatively constant over time, unless specific intervention is sought. Therefore, families will likely deal with bereavement in ways similar to how they dealt with the terminal phase of illness. If families function in such a way that makes redefining more likely during the terminal phase of illness, then the same conditions will make it easier for surviving members to redefine their altered situation in bereavement.

Participation in a hospice care program is associated with more positive bereavement outcome in family members following the death of a patient from cancer (Parkes, 1985). All families in this study, however, were involved in supportive care programs. Since there was much variation among families in how they managed the transition of fading away, it is important to recognize that hospice participation alone is not sufficient to facilitate optimal bereavement. In conclusion, attention must be given to how families manage the transition; in particular, how family members redefine themselves and their situation. It is important to allow bereaved family members to tell their story, to reflect on the dimensions of fading away, and to encourage conversation about the patient and how he or she redefined the situation.

Living and Learning the Reality of a Loved One's Dying: Traumatic Stress and Cognitive Processing in Anticipatory Grief

3

Therese A. Rando, Ph.D.

Introduction

Thanatologists have debated the merits—and in some cases the very existence—of anticipatory grief intermittently since 1944, when Erich Lindemann first introduced the concept at the close of his classic article, "Symptomatology and Management of Acute Grief." In those few sentences he initiated decades of controversy by observing that the *threat* of death or separation could itself initiate a bereavement reaction. In such instances a person could be so concerned with adjustment after the potential death of a loved one that all the phases of grief are undergone: specifically, "depression, heightened preoccupation with the departed, a review of all the forms of death which might befall him, and anticipation of the modes of readjustment which might be necessitated by it" (pp. 147–148). However, such advance preparation is not without some cost. While it can serve as a safeguard should the death actually occur, it may inhibit continued involvement if the death does not occur. Lindemann presented the case in which a wife was so concerned with the possible death of her soldier husband that she effectively emotionally emancipated herself from him, such that when he did return alive she demanded an immediate divorce. Lindemann interpreted that the wife no longer had any emotional investment in her husband; her ensuing readjustment had mandated that she direct herself toward new involvements and interactions. What was not said, but what I and others would submit, is that such premature detachment is not necessarily an example of anticipatory grief per se, but a perfect example of anticipatory grief gone awry.

Since the publication of that article, there have been significant controversies and contradictory research findings regarding the phenomenon. (See Rando, 1986, for a discussion of a majority of these.) However, careful analysis reveals that these are often quite well explained by conceptual confusions, clinical misassumptions and misconceptions, inadequate research designs, inconsistent definitions and poor operationalizations of the concept, and semantics contributing to the impression that the differences are more real than apparent.

These discrepancies notwithstanding, the general consensus is that there is *some* experience that both the dying individual and his or her loved ones undergo if and when they have accurate information about the reality of the illness and its implications and choose to pay attention to it. Certainly, there would be much disagreement over what the precise nature, extent, breadth, determining factors, and impact of these experiences might be. However, living with the life-threatening or terminal illness of oneself or one's loved one constitutes a potent kind of experience that significantly impacts upon the individual; influences his or her subjective existence; presents him or her with myriad physical and psychosocial losses; gives rise to certain needs, feelings, thoughts, experiences, and behaviors; and demands extensive assumptive world revision consequent to the massive disarticulation between the way the world now is and the way it "should be," according to that individual's assumptive world, i.e., the set of assumptions, expectations, and beliefs he or she has developed about the self and the world on the basis of previous experience.

With that as a fundamental assumption, and following a brief outline of points about anticipatory grief, I will examine two aspects of the anticipatory grief experience which I feel have been seriously overlooked: its essence as a trauma and its cognitive processes with their teaching functions and stimulation of necessary internal and external change. Throughout, I will assert the clinical need for caregivers to incorporate these two elements into the traditional anticipatory grief framework and target them in their treatment strategies. For purposes of clarity of instruction, I will restrict my remarks to the anticipatory grief of the loved ones of the dying. I do believe the points to be equally relevant to the anticipatory grief experience of the dying person him or herself, and the reader can extrapolate these as appropriate for that individual.

The Phenomenon of Anticipatory Grief

In an earlier work (Rando, 1986), I attempted to offer a comprehensive analysis of the complex and multidimensional phenomenon of anticipatory grief; providing an operational definition for it, delineating its component processes, discussing its associated issues, differentiating among the principals involved in it, considering developmental concerns of those grappling with it, and identifying specific interventions and coping strategies for facilitating a healthy experience of it. Recognizing that there has been much debate in the field, I nonetheless maintain that the following eight points are essential for a caregiver to comprehend and must be accounted for in any treatment intervention aimed at those whose loved one is dying. (For a full discussion of each point, please see my earlier work.)

1. Anticipatory grief is a complex and multidimensional experience that can be defined as follows: "Anticipatory grief is the phenomenon encompassing the processes of mourning, coping, interaction, planning, and psychosocial reorganization that are stimulated and begun in part in response to the awareness of the impending death of a loved one and the recognition of associated losses in the past, present, and future. It mandates a delicate balance among the mutually conflicting demands of simultaneously holding onto, letting go of, and drawing closer to the dying loved one."

2. In the area of anticipatory grief, the caregiver has the golden opportunity to utilize primary prevention strategies and to make

therapeutic interventions that may facilitate a more positive post-death bereavement experience for the survivor-to-be. In a loved one's dying process responded to by healthy anticipatory grief, the numerous overwhelming assaults and harmful consequences of sudden death are avoided, specifically those related to the traumatization of the survivor and violent instantaneous shattering of his or her assumptive world, as well as those associated with losing a loved one without anticipation (Rando, 1996). In terms of an illness experience, healthy anticipatory grief minimizes, if not eliminates, the unfinished business, premature detachment, poor communication and interaction with the dying loved one, and lack of appropriate anticipation, each of which is known to predispose to poor post-death bereavement outcomes. Interventions in these and other areas during the anticipatory grief period can prevent problems in post-death grief and mourning from developing; later interventions can only attempt to remedy difficulties that already have occurred.

3. Anticipatory grief is not merely conventional post-death grief begun earlier. It is different in nature and impact, physiology, and the experiences of ambivalence, denial, hope, endpoints, and acceleration. Anticipatory grief is not the same as forewarning of loss or length of illness, and cannot be assumed to be present merely because a warning or terminal illness diagnosis has been given, a particular length of time has elapsed from the onset of illness until actual death, or the family member is aware of and not denying the advance of the death of the loved one. In other words, it does not necessarily occur by itself as a result of knowledge of anticipated loss. Reacting to the pain of a loved one's terminal illness and impending death, while part of anticipatory grief, is not by itself sufficient to meet the healthy experience of anticipatory grief that necessarily involves numerous active processes of mourning.

4. The term *anticipatory grief* is a misnomer. *Anticipatory* suggests that one is grieving solely for anticipated as opposed to past and current losses as well, and *grief* implies to some the necessity of a complete detachment from one's dying loved one as opposed to one's previous hopes for and with that person in the future. If

inappropriate premature detachment from the dying-yet-still-living loved one does occur, anticipatory grief has gone awry since crucial components of it (i.e., the interactional processes with the dying patient) are not being realized.

5. Anticipatory grief is multidimensional. It defines itself across two perspectives—the dying person him or herself and the ones who are emotionally involved with that person in some way; three time foci—past, present, and future losses; and three classes of influencing variables: (a) psychological factors—including characteristics pertaining to the nature and meaning of the person and the relationship to be lost, personal characteristics of the anticipatory griever, and characteristics pertaining to the illness and type of death with which the anticipatory griever must contend; (b) social factors—including characteristics of the dying patient's knowledge and response to the illness and ultimate death, characteristics of the family and its members' responses to the illness and impending death, and general socioeconomic and environmental factors; and (c) physiological factors associated with the anticipatory griever.

6. The experience of anticipatory grievers when a loved one is terminally ill typically involves monumental confrontations with a number of issues. These include: (a) powerlessness, fear, uncertainty, and confusion; (b) violations of the assumptive world; (c) ongoing losses; (d) personal depletion from the stress arising from demands for major readaptions and investments of self, time, and finances; (e) long-term family disruption and disorganization; (f) balancing of opposing needs, competing demands, discordant roles, clashing responsibilities, and antagonistic tasks; (g) traumatizing physical, emotional, and social experiences during the illness; and (h) major emotional reactions of guilt, sorrow and depression, anger and hostility, and anxiety.

7. Anticipatory grief that is therapeutic in nature prompts engagement in three interrelated sets of processes that facilitate one another. They take place within the griever; between the griever and the dying loved one; and within the familial and social contexts. The second area involves the dying loved one, and invalidates the belief that anticipatory grief necessarily must lead to

premature detachment from the loved one or cause the relationship with him or her to deteriorate. All of the subprocesses in that sphere imply continued involvement with the dying loved one, with some actually serving to intensify the attachment and improve the relationship. Although critics may construe anticipatory grief and continued involvement with the dying patient as seemingly opposite processes, this is quite untrue in the model offered here. The three categories of processes composing anticipatory grief comprise: (a) Individual Intrapsychic Processes—these include four interrelated sets of subprocesses, each with its own components: awareness of and gradual accommodation to the threat; affective processes; cognitive processes; and planning for the future; (b) Interactional Process with the Dying Patient— these include three interrelated sets of subprocesses, each with its own components: directing attention, energy, and behavior toward the dying patient; resolution of personal relationship with the dying patient; and helping the dying patient; and (c) Familial and Social Processes.

8. As pertains to the survivors' post-death bereavement experience, there appears to be an optimum amount of anticipatory grief in which to engage. Too little or too much can compromise the survivor's adjustment. Additionally, despite all of the therapeutic benefits of healthy anticipatory grief, it is not without some costs (Rando, 1986).

Anticipatory Grief as an Experience of Traumatic Stress

I believe that the period of time and experiences during a loved one's dying legitimately present the anticipatory griever with circumstances generating reactions that meet the diagnostic criteria for significant posttraumatic stress symptomology, if not, in fact, full-blown Posttraumatic Stress Disorder (PTSD), according to the DSM-IV (*Diagnostic and Statistical Manual of Mental Disorders*; American Psychiatric Association, 1994). This is a very important realization because the concepts of traumatic stress are quite useful in informing us further about the anticipatory grief experience for those undergoing it. For this reason, I will specify below how the experiences of anticipatory grief taking place within the context of the loved one's dying meet the standard diagnostic criteria, and I will suggest several important implications that derive from this.

Briefly, the anticipatory griever meets the diagnostic criteria because he or she has been and is continuing to be: exposed to a traumatic event (i.e., the loved one's dying) in which the griever "experienced, witnessed, or was confronted with an event or events that involved actual or threatened death or serious injury, or a threat to the physical integrity of self or others" (p. 427) and the griever's "response involved intense fear, helplessness, or horror" (p. 428).

The second set of criteria requires that the traumatic event be persistently reexperienced in one or more of the following ways, each of which is not uncommon during and after the anticipatory grief experience: (a) recurrent and intrusive distressing recollections of the event, including images, thoughts, or perceptions; (b) recurrent distressing dreams of the event; (c) acting or feeling as if the traumatic event were recurring (includes a sense of reliving the experience, illusions, hallucinations, and dissociative flashback episodes, including those which occur on awakening or when intoxicated); (d) intense psychological distress at exposure to internal or external cues that symbolize or resemble an aspect of the traumatic event; or (e) physiological reactivity on exposure to internal or external cues that symbolize or resemble an aspect of the traumatic event (p. 428).

The third set of criteria pertains to the persistent avoidance of stimuli associated with the trauma and numbing of general responsiveness not present before the trauma, as indicated by three or more of the following: (a) efforts to avoid thoughts, feelings, or conversations associated with the trauma; (b) efforts to avoid activities, places, or people that arouse recollections of the trauma; (c) inability to recall an important aspect of the trauma; (d) markedly diminished interest or participation in significant activities; (e) feeling of detachment or estrangement from others; (f) restricted range of affect; or (g) sense of a foreshortened future (p. 428).

The fourth set of criteria involves persistent symptoms of increased arousal (not present before the trauma of the loved one's dy-

ing), as indicated by two or more of the following: (a) difficulty fall-
ing or staying asleep; (b) irritability or outbursts of anger; (c) difficulty concentrating; (d) hypervigilance; or (e) exaggerated startle
response (p. 428).

Caregivers familiar with the pre- and post-death experiences of
anticipatory grievers will readily recognize the vast majority of these
diagnostic symptoms as typical reactions in those who are contending with losing, or already having lost, a loved one to the ravages of a
terminal illness. Clearly, not all anticipatory grievers develop full-
blown PTSD. And, certainly, many who do develop a number of
these symptoms fail to meet the other two diagnostic criteria of duration of symptomatology of the second through fourth sets of symptoms lasting more than one month, and the disturbance causing
clinically significant distress or impairment in social, occupational,
or other important areas of functioning (p. 429). Nevertheless, it is
vitally important to develop a sensitivity to the traumatic nature of
the anticipatory grief experience—it is a veritable trauma to observe
and attend a loved one's dying—and to be cognizant of, and respon-
sive to, the traumatic stress that results from it.

Caregivers must maintain an awareness of the horrific nature of
the loved one's dying, along with a deep appreciation of the frustrat-
ing sense of helplessness, fear, and eventual anger that accompany
witnessing a dearly loved person slip away without being able to prevent it. It means helping the anticipatory griever work through and
master the many traumatic affects to which this experience gives rise,
including the overwhelming and disorganizing anxiety with which
the anticipatory griever so typically exists for extended periods of
time. Unfortunately, this emotion is frequently overlooked by
caregivers who tend to focus more of their attention on that person's
depression or sorrow instead.

Responding to anticipatory grief as a trauma also entails recognizing and then responding to the fact that an inherent part of its
distress comes from the mutually contradictory demands of simultaneously holding onto and letting go of the dying loved one. Distress
also comes from the anticipatory griever's attempting to contend with
and balance a host of antagonistic tasks, clashing responsibilities, and
discordant roles. The caregiver must design interventions to enable

the anticipatory griever to interact therapeutically with a loved one who, while still living, is also slowly dying and dealing with his or her own anticipatory grief, assorted coping mechanisms, and emotions, all of which have been marshaled to manage the stress of losing the self, the world, and everything and everyone in it.

Therapeutic strategies must specifically address the reality that there can be no greater trauma than helplessly watching your loved one permanently, irretrievably and, in most cases, unwillingly being pulled away; knowing the terror that the unknown can bring; forcing oneself to come to closure with that loved one; seeing the robbing of that loved one's personal control and the massive violations of his or her assumptive world; viewing the ongoing losses, physical and spiritual suffering, and the myriad of emotions with which most dying individuals contend at some point; and ultimately, the anticipatory griever's saying goodbye to that loved one and tolerating the awareness that he or she will die while the griever continues to exist.

The treatment goals for the anticipatory griever and the traumatized individual are basically the same. In both, caregivers are called to enable the achievement of cognitive completion with emotional release so that the person can go on in the new world in a meaningfully healthy and appropriate fashion. The person must be connected to others and have worked through associated emotions; mourned relevant losses; integrated memories, affects, images, behaviors, and physical sensations of the experience; revised the assumptive world as necessary; and placed the trauma as one element within the totality of one's past, present, and future; and formed a new identity that reflects accommodation of the associated losses and survival of the experience.

Further support for the view of shared characteristics between posttraumatic stress and the experiences and sequelae of the anticipatory grief experience comes from Raphael (1981). In a paper on personal disaster, she describes intensely distressing, possibly catastrophic personal experiences which, despite being relatively ordinary and possibly inevitable events of human life, are calamitous to those who are involved and predispose to what is now generically termed posttraumatic stress. Specifically, she identifies three types of personal disaster: bereavement following the death of a loved one; a personal experience of major disaster; or a life-threatening accident or illness. Raphael observes how events are more "disastrous" to the human being when they are "undesirable as opposed to desirable; exit as opposed to entrance; loss as opposed to gain; high distress as opposed to low distress; associated with a high as opposed to low level of change; unable to be prevented or controlled, as opposed to preventable or controllable; unanticipated as opposed to anticipated" (p. 185).

With the exception of the last factor, it is quite clear that the anticipatory griever's experience during the dying of his or her loved one meets Raphael's criteria for being enormously personally disastrous. At least six of the seven high-risk factors are present, with the seventh one frequently in attendance at the beginning of the experience, if not at selected points throughout. Raphael notes that personal disaster precipitating trauma for the individual—whether in the face of massive stress from the extraordinary or the ordinary calamities of life—involves five key responses, all of which are found in the anticipatory grief experience and require intervention. These include: shock and denial; distress; helplessness; death and destruction; and images.

Caregivers must therefore approach the anticipatory griever from both the traumatology and thanatology perspectives. We must work toward mastery of whatever traumatic stress is present and utilize suitable interventions identified as effective with posttraumatic stress, in general, as well as enable healthy grieving and accommodation of associated losses through the use of appropriate interventions for either complicated or uncomplicated mourning. Only with the integration of both types of interventions will the anticipatory mourner be appropriately served. Reliance on one without the other will most assuredly leave treatment incomplete.

It is important for the reader to be aware that there are some in the traumatology field who will not favor the application of the PTSD diagnostic category to personal disasters such as bereavement, and strongly believe that it would do a disservice to the concept. This perspective stresses that PTSD categorization be reserved for more catastrophic types of traumas, such as major disasters or events that are outside of the normal range of human experience, such as the

Oklahoma City bombing, the Holocaust, or participation in the Vietnam War. Caregivers need to be aware of the reasons behind the reluctance on the part of some traumatologists to "share" their diagnostic category. Notwithstanding this, the usefulness of the conceptualization of anticipatory bereavement (and conventional post-death acute grief, as well) as trauma still stands.

The Role of Cognitive Processes in Anticipatory Grief

The Omission of Cognition as a Focus of Concern in Thanatology

Not unlike a similar omission made regarding conventional post-death grief and mourning, another aspect of the anticipatory grief experience which I believe has been ignored pertains to the overfocus on the emotional or affective components of the experience to the relative diminution, if not neglect, of the cognitive aspects. In other words, what has tended to be somewhat lost in clinical thanatology's various analyses of bereavement—whether anticipatory or post-death—is the fact that the human being is a cognitive animal as well as an emotional one, and will need to address experiences on that level along with a feeling one. In fact, the inability to successfully process experiences in the cognitive domain and work them through to make sense, and eliminate or markedly reduce any cognitive dissonance that may be present, will create significant emotional distress for the person, oftentimes exerting a pressure for certain behaviors or acting out in response.

The importance of the cognitive sphere has been explicitly recognized throughout history, from ancient philosophy through Festinger's (1957) seminal work on cognitive dissonance up to contemporary times as evidenced by the popularity of cognitive and behavioral approaches to mental health intervention. Unfortunately, it has not transferred well to the specialization of clinical thanatology. There, with the exception of a relative handful of writers who focus upon meaning reconstruction (e.g., Neimeyer, 1997), personal construct adaptation (e.g., Woodfield and Viney, 1984–1985), psychosocial transitions (e.g., Parkes, 1988), assumptive world revision (e.g.,

Rando, 1993), or relearning of the world (e.g., Attig, 1996), proportionally little has been articulated about the importance of cognitive processes during or following the death of a loved one. This has translated into the typical frontline caregiver's spending scant, if any, time on these issues in his or her practice with the dying, their loved ones, and post-death mourners. It also has left these parties at a relative disadvantage.

The remainder of this chapter will examine the nature and role of cognitive processes in anticipatory and post-death bereavement. It will take the position that these processes are necessary for and facilitative of healthy adjustment in bereaved individuals.

Types of Cognitive Processes in Bereavement

There are two sets of cognitive processes associated with bereavement, whether anticipatory or post-death. The first set relates to the individual's learning about the reality of the loved one's impending or actual loss and appreciation of its implications. The second set, contingent upon the success of the first, pertains specifically to revision of the assumptive world, the necessity for adopting new ways of being in the external world, and the formation of a new identity incorporating the changes demanded by the deterioration in or loss of the loved one.

The caregiver must fully understand that the cognitive adjustment to loss influences affective or emotional adjustment and vice versa. It is just as necessary and requires equal attention. Without appropriate cognitive change, the mourner simply cannot go forward in a healthy fashion, regardless of how much emotional processing has been completed. Review of the literature on coming to terms with major negative life events suggests that cognitions and emotions are equally essential, and that the working-through process involves dynamic interplay between them (Tait and Silver, 1989).

How We Are Taught About Loss: The Gradual Erosion of Disbelief

While we may be able to acknowledge the fact of a loved one's fatal diagnosis relatively soon after we first are informed of it, it will take us considerably longer to be able to fully appreciate and actually internalize its reality and implications. Denial is typically cited as the reason for the lag time between what we know in our head and our transmittal of it to our gut, where we finally realize it at the deepest level. However, while denial certainly may play a part—and sometimes a considerable one—in accounting for this delay, disbelief is equally as potent a variable, if not more so. What traditionally has been termed "denial" is often less an active contradiction of reality than it actually is disbelief occasioned by inadequate information (Bowlby, 1980).

In other words, it is not as if we are able to grasp the reality of our loved one's dying and then on some level choose not to do so. Rather, we simply are unable to grasp that reality for some period of time. It is utterly too elusive; we cannot sustain it. If someone has been an integral part of our physical, emotional, social existences, it will take us considerable time to be able to bend our minds around the fact that he or she is not going to be there anymore. It is something that we can only comprehend a little at a time, not because we are denying, but because we cannot conceive of the world without our loved one. It is not part of our reality, nor of our assumptive world, not to have this person alive in our life. It will only be over time, as we are gradually taught through the experiences of the terminal illness and its (hopefully) healthy anticipatory grief processes, that we truly start to learn the reality that the one we love is dying.

How are we taught that a loved one is dying? How do we decondition ourselves from expecting him or her to continue to be in our lives? How do we learn the truth that there is no future with our loved one, at least not in the sense of life as we have known it? This process may be easier to discern by first examining how it occurs after a sudden, unanticipated death.

Cognitive Processing in Post-Death Bereavement

After a sudden death, the survivor, unable to grasp the change and its implications all at once, only learns in small increments that the loved one is truly dead. It is the survivor's pain of needing, yearning, and striving to reunite with his or her loved one in countless ways—to hold, touch, hear, and see that loved one—and then repeatedly having these needs excruciatingly unrequited that imparts the lesson. As the survivor reaches out in the middle of the night to touch the loved one, the pain of the sudden awareness that his hand only touches air, because his spouse died two weeks ago from a heart attack, teaches him. When it is 2:30 in the afternoon and the mother hears the school bus, looks up expectantly to see her child bound into the house, and then is nauseated by remembering that she buried him a month ago after he was hit by a drunk driver, her agony teaches her, too.

What does the experience of the pain and agony—occasioned by their confrontations with the absences of their loved ones—teach these survivors? It teaches them that, despite their most fervent wishes to the contrary, their loved one is dead. It takes thousands, if not hundreds of thousands, of these types of lessons, of these repeated experiences of bumping up against the loved one's absence, before the survivor really learns that the loved one is truly gone. The survivor gradually learns not to have the same needs for that person anymore and ultimately makes appropriate revisions in his or her assumptive world and the necessary adaptations in his or her external world to accommodate to the physical absence of that loved one. It is only then that the survivor will not reach out for the person anymore in the middle of the night or expect to see the loved one once again coming into the house at 2:30 after the school bus rolls by.

The learning occasioned in the first set of cognitive processes, which has taught the person about the actual death of the loved one and its implications, facilitates the second set of cognitive processes associated with readjustments in the assumptive world, the external world, and the sense of identity. In particular, in the assumptive world, the survivor ultimately has to relinquish all of the specific expectations, assumptions, and beliefs that were predicated upon the continued existence of the loved one, and to take on new ones appropriate to the new world without that person. In other words, all of the assumptive world elements specific to the deceased must be relinquished, and insofar as the death and its consequences violated any global assumptions, these must be relinquished or revised, or new ones must be incorporated.

Correspondingly, in the external world, the survivor has to find alternative ways of meeting the needs the deceased previously filled, or else to change his or her desires for what was previously needed from the deceased and now is unfulfilled. Roles, skills, behaviors, and relationships may have to be relinquished, taken on, or modified to compensate for what is lost in the loved one's death. The changes in all these internal and external areas ultimately lead to the formation of a new identity or sense of self. This is part of the transformative power of grief and mourning.

There are four types of theories of cognitive adaptation to threatening or traumatic events that can be brought to bear in understanding this second set of cognitive processes in bereavement. They address a number of cardinal issues that are associated both with trauma and the dying of a loved one, including: disarticulation of the way the world is and the way one's assumptive world maintains that it should be; cognitive processing; integration of new and old; secondary losses; traumatic stress; victimization; and searches for meaning and mastery. The theories respond quite well to the inherent traumatic stress found in even the most healthy anticipatory grief. Each of them suggests targets of interventions and strategies that must be incorporated clinically into interventions in bereavement, whether anticipatory or post-death.

The four types of theories of cognitive adaptation to threatening or traumatic events are:

1. Parkes' (1988) revision of the assumptive world following psychosocial transitions, and Woodfield and Viney's (1984–1985) work on personal construct dislocation and adaptation in bereavement;
2. Horowitz's (1986) cognitive processing aspects of the stress response syndrome and integration of memories and responses, meanings, new assumptive world, and new sense of self;
3. Taylor's (1983) theory of cognitive adjustment to threatening events centering on the search for meaning in the experience, the attempt to regain mastery over the event in particular and over one's life in general, and the effort to restore self-esteem through self-enhancing evaluations;

4. Janoff-Bulman's (1985) theory of the necessity to rebuild shattered assumptive worlds following victimization, specifically after the losses of the belief in personal invulnerability, the perception of the world as meaningful, and the perception of oneself as positive.

Cognitive Processing in Anticipatory Grief

As noted above, cognitive processing and education take place not only in conventional post-death bereavement, but during life-threatening and terminal illness as well. The anticipatory griever learns through confrontations with the vicissitudes of the loved one's illness, and through the experience of repeated frustrations of the need to see the loved one not be sick, or at least to improve. A progressively deepening awareness develops of the seriousness of the illness and its implications as the realization occurs that certain hopes about recovery or stabilization are not being actualized. At some point in time there is a rehearsing of the death and its consequences, with attempts made by the anticipatory griever to, in part, adjust in advance. During the illness, experiences such as the wife's being forced to attend a social function alone, or the children's having to accommodate to their mother's missing their award ceremonies, not only reinforce the current reality, but portend a small bit of what the world will be like after the death. In a very real fashion, the anticipatory griever starts to get an indication of what the world without the loved one will be like by extrapolating from the illness experiences that foreshadow the permanent absence in the future. He or she becomes partially socialized into the bereaved role through this time of anticipatory grief (Gerber, 1974).

This new information gradually starts to supplant the old assumptions, expectations, and beliefs about this person, such as their being healthy, having a long-term future, and being able to be with the anticipatory griever as he or she wants and needs. When the loved one relies more on medication for symptom control, as the anticipatory griever witnesses that the extent of disability is increasing, as yet another relapse ends an increasingly shorter remission—these are all experiences that teach the anticipatory griever that the dying loved one is truly seriously ill; that this is not a nightmare but a reality that must be dealt with, despite intense needs otherwise. Each of these little lessons erodes the anticipatory griever's disbelief until at some point he or she truly comprehends and believes the reality of the loved one's dying. The anticipatory griever has been provided sufficient data through these lessons so that disbelief gives way to recognition of the reality and its implications. The information he or she may have intellectually acknowledged initially at the time of diagnosis now has been internalized at a gut level, the journey from head to heart fueled by repeated confrontations with the illness and the consequent demands for changes in the anticipatory griever's assumptive world, ways of being in the external world, and sense of self.

Along the way, the individual's engagement in healthy anticipatory grief can facilitate the gradual coming to grips with the reality of the impending death. Depending upon the specific factors influencing the person's anticipatory grief at that point in time, other assumptive world revisions are made in addition to those pertaining to the loved one. These, in turn, stimulate changes in the anticipatory griever's ways of being in the external world, which in this case not only means learning to be in the world without the loved one present there as before, but also includes learning how to relate to the loved one in new ways appropriate to his or her new reality as a life-threatened or terminally ill person. This is where the anticipatory grief components of the interactional processes with the dying patient assume significant importance. Here the anticipatory griever directs attention, energy, and behaviors toward the dying loved one, works on resolving the personal relationship with him or her, and undertakes behaviors to help the loved one as a dying patient.

A number of other cognitive processes occur during anticipatory grief. These have to do with various anticipatory griever responses to the loved one's illness, as well as with planning and problem-solving strategies. Among these ancillary cognitive processes are: experiencing heightened preoccupation with and concern for the loved one; attempting to crystallize memories and to construct a composite image of the loved one to endure after death; bargaining with God or fate; recollecting earlier losses and other related experiences that have been revived by the loved one's dying; contemplating one's own death and the deaths of other loved ones; developing a philosophy about how to cope with the loved one's remaining time; considering what the future will be like without the loved one and experiencing associated reactions to it; and anticipating and planning for the pre-death and post-death future in terms of losses and changes, practical and social considerations, and fulfillment of the loved one's and other survivors-to-be's needs and preferences.

Caregivers must come to appreciate and capacitate the functions of the two sets of cognitive processes in anticipatory grief. They are necessary for and facilitative of both the recognition of the reality of the loved one's dying and the subsequent undertaking of healthy changes and internal and external readjustments to respond appropriately to it. A number of ancillary cognitive processes attend anticipatory grief as well and should be supported by caregivers to whatever extent is suitable.

Summary

This chapter has identified two frequently overlooked aspects of the anticipatory grief experience—its essence as a trauma and its cognitive processes with their teaching functions and stimulation of necessary internal and external change. For comprehensive treatment of anticipatory grief, the traditional approaches to intervention should be augmented with caregiver recognition of the importance of these two elements and corresponding incorporation of techniques and strategies focused upon therapeutic response to them as suggested above.

Hard Decisions in Hard Times: Making Ethical Choices During Prolonged Illness

4

David M. Price, M.Div., Ph.D.

Every medical treatment decision is an ethical decision. That is to say, every such decision is an answer to a *should* question:

"Should I undergo another round of chemotherapy?"
"Should we bring Grandma home to die?"
"Should we begin dialysis?"
"What should we do about this low blood count?"

A sound answer to each question depends on technical information or expert advice. But none can be answered by reference to technical knowledge alone. Each decision has a value component. Each turns, in significant part, upon some notion of what is worth what; that is why every medical decision is an ethical decision.

In the course of a prolonged illness, the patient and (usually) his or her close family members or friends will make many such ethical decisions. They will make them in conjunction with health care professionals who bring to the decisionmaking relevant knowledge and experience and, one hopes, skillful, empathic support through the decision-making process.

Patients and family or friends will need such support, not only because these decisions tend to be difficult and couched in unfamiliar terms, but because the decisions must be made in the context of grief. A prolonged illness, even if it is not perceived as necessarily ending in death, nonetheless entails prolonged grief. A long, often progressive illness typically includes loss of well-being, vigor, function, social status and self-image. Responses to such losses are profound, whether they are losses in one's self or in a partner, parent, child or sibling.

Sudden death or death after a brief illness compresses grief. There are relatively few health care decisions to make and they tend to seem largely apart from real life. In a brief, fatal illness, survivors are actually excused from making some decisions. Other decisions and major pursuits are postponed. Life seems to stand still. One takes time out for a brief illness and for acute grief. By contrast, in prolonged illness, life must go on and health care decisions that must be made are made in the midst of life *and* in the midst of grief. Moreover, these decisions tend to be more complicated in terms of their impact on ongoing family patterns and interests:

"Should we put Mother in a nursing home?
"Should Kenny be taken off the ventilator?"
"Is it right to let Dad make this decision about amputation?"
"Should we feed her by mouth even though we know she could get pneumonia?"

As these questions or ethical dilemmas illustrate, many health care decisions are choices among "least worst" alternatives. Accordingly, the guilt that is a familiar component of grief can easily find a focus. Guilt, whether real or imagined, is no friend of sound and timely decisionmaking. It is easy to see how the interaction of grief and ethical decisionmaking cuts both ways: the nature of the decisions prompts grief responses, while aspects of grieving complicate decisionmaking.

This chapter focuses upon the kinds of health care decisions that face patients and their loved ones at the end of life. The intention is to show how health professionals and other support persons often make these decisions more difficult than they need to be and to identify a few basic ideas for how to facilitate responsible health care decisionmaking by those who are experiencing major loss in the context of prolonged and progressive illness.

Shared Decisionmaking

Important health care decisions tend to be shared decisions; more than one person is usually involved in the process. This appears to be true both in the sense that it is proper that it be so, and in the sense that that is what generally happens.

Decisions are shared in two dimensions. First, the clinician (the physician or other health professional) and the patient (or surrogate for the patient, if the patient is incapacitated) share decisionmaking in a process known as *informed consent.* The clinician lays out options, provides explanations and predictions and, perhaps, offers advice. The patient or surrogate assimilates, analyzes and evaluates. The process is properly and, indeed, necessarily a dialogue. It ends with a decision to which both parties agree, a plan of care which they then implement cooperatively. Though this process is often flawed and occasionally is so flawed as to support a judgment that there was no informed consent at all, this shared decisionmaking is the ethical (and legal) ideal. Most of the time, clinicians, patients and families manage a rough approximation of the ideal.

The second dimension of shared decisionmaking is what happens between the patient (or surrogate) and his or her significant support people. Patients and principal family caretakers rarely act alone, despite the fact that they might be fully within their rights to do so. Even when one member of a family is clearly authorized to make decisions, it almost invariably happens that others are informed, involved and consulted. Dying mothers and fathers frequently reshape their decisions to accommodate the sensibilities and preferences of their grown children. Spouses typically take each other into account and do not act on their individual preferences alone. Even deeply estranged family members commonly make room for each other in family councils. The sole signature on a consent form belies the typical array of stakeholders and the fact that, as hard as it may be to do so, they do tend to acknowledge and include each other when there are important health care decisions to make on behalf of a common loved one.

In two senses, then, health care decisions at the end of life ordinarily come out of a process of shared decisionmaking. Not only do patients or their surrogates decide in conjunction with professional advisors, but those who are bound by familial duty or affection generally consult broadly as important end-of-life decisions are made.

They do so for a variety of reasons. The one most often is articulated is, "I want this to be something they can all live with." It would not be too far off to rephrase this sentiment as, "I want to decide in such a way as to not unduly complicate their grieving."

Responsibility

People faced with difficult health care decisions are often most impressive, even inspiring, in their bravery and selfless devotion to duty. The young parents of a child with devastating congenital problems who, despite the fact that nothing in their short lives has prepared them for this responsibility, learn what they have to know, master their urge to flee and face into an ordeal that one might expect would overwhelm them. A daughter manages to put aside her own deeply held preferences in order to honor her father's wishes. A husband who is very nervous about bringing his dying wife home does it anyway. The neighbor of a woman who has no family volunteers to become the legal guardian in order to authorize her friend's removal from life support. To work with such people as they make these decisions is a great and humbling privilege.

A few families are seriously dysfunctional and some patient surrogates are thoroughly irresponsible. Occasionally, decisionmakers or whole families manage to evade responsibility in ways that defy the most conscientious efforts to assist and support. There are passive-aggressive personalities who make a pretense of responsibility while the patient languishes and clinician frustration mounts. Fortunately, these are relatively rare.

All of what follows in this discussion of ethical decisionmaking as it impacts upon grieving persons presumes that most patients and most family members are basically responsible, and that, with proper assistance, they will engage in good faith efforts to discern the right thing to do.

Sound Decisionmaking

It is possible to identify certain features of a good decisionmaking process without requiring subscription to any particular methodology or ethical theory. Generally approvable marks of sound decisionmaking include:

Adequate information. Good decisions require good information. The very first step in any sound decisionmaking process is to assess whether the relevant information is reliable and complete. "Information" includes both facts and interpretations, both description and judgments. The perceived adequacy of the information may depend in significant measure on the reputation of those who have gathered the facts and made the interpretations.

Appropriate identification of alternatives. A frequent and serious mistake in decisionmaking is to proceed to make one's choice between two or three perceived options when, in fact, more care or imagination would have revealed additional alternatives. Sometimes the choice is framed in a way that distorts or obscures the nature of the real options. It is possible to do everything else flawlessly and still miss the best alternative because it was never identified or adequately articulated.

Identification of decisionmakers. It may not be obvious who should make certain decisions. This uncertainty can derail an otherwise good process. Shared decisionmaking as discussed above entails an often delicate apportionment of decisionmaking power or complementary aspects of a complex decision.

Identification of Stakeholders. For many decisions, persons or organizations who would not be identified as rightful decisionmakers nonetheless have a discernable interest in the outcome. Interests may include money, prestige, ego, ideological stance or expected courtesies. Full understanding of the social, political, organizational, and economic context within which the decision process unfolds requires attention to interested parties as well as to those who have direct decisionmaking roles.

Tolerance as affirmative respect. Those who share responsibility for a joint decision may or may not come from the same place ethically. If they approach the decision in basically the same way (for example, from the perspective of "rights" and centrality of the principles of personal liberty), then decisionmaking is apt to go smoothly. However, it commonly happens that those who share decisionmaking proceed from different starting points or along divergent paths. In such cases, sound and efficient decisionmaking depends upon a common commitment to tolerance and respectful listening.

We seem to be becoming a more tolerant people, despite signs of a worldwide resurgence of religious fanaticism and ethnic jingoism. Most of us seem to be more aware of pluralism and less certain that *our* cultural perspective is the only one worth notice. One hopes that this modern awareness does not lead to a moral relativism in which one opinion is thought to be as good as any and morality is equated with mere preference. Tolerance is a much more robust and demanding virtue. It respects persons, especially as they attempt to make principled decisions. True tolerance succeeds not by devaluing the issues or traditions that divide us, but by affirmatively respecting those who differ in good faith.

Clarity about key terms and concepts. Good decisionmaking is marked by precision of language, especially with respect to those words that are central to moral reasoning, emotionally "loaded" or heavy with obscure authority. In short, good decisionmaking is careful to either avoid or to define exactly those kinds of evocative terms and allusions that are deliberately used by advertising writers and campaigning politicians. In the language of morals, as in political speech, there is a time and place for rhetorical flourish and emotional appeals. But when there are important decisions to make in difficult circumstances, sound decisions depend in part upon a good-faith effort to be as clear as possible about what is meant by key words and important ideas.

The above six marks of good decisionmaking are all the more important when some of the parties to the analysis and choosing are simultaneously coping with significant loss. If prolonged illness means "living with grief," it means deciding with grief. This realization underscores the importance of optimizing the decisionmaking process along the lines just suggested.

Common Decision Points in Prolonged Illness

The balance of this chapter is devoted to some of the common decisions faced by or on behalf of patients with prolonged and ultimately fatal illnesses. Against the background of earlier discussions of the shared nature of health care decisionmaking and the characteristics of good decisionmaking process, we now proceed to examine some practices that militate against good decisionmaking, entailing added stress and, perhaps, longer term complications for grieving patients and their families.

We will also consider alternative strategies consistent with the foregoing marks of good decisionmaking. These are potential interventions by which helping professionals and friends can make hard choices, not easy, but more satisfying and more healing. Assuring sound and confident health care decisions is a way of facilitating, rather than complicating, the adaptive process known as grief.

Foregoing Cure-Oriented Treatment. At some point in many prolonged and progressing illnesses, there comes a point (or points) when those who share responsibility for the treatment plan will ask, "Should we stop our efforts to 'beat' the disease in favor of efforts to promote quality of life?" This development begins with an acknowledgment that the likelihood of cure or remission is fading and that the patient and the therapies are being overmastered by the disease. In the terms of grief dynamics, denial and bargaining give way to acceptance. This is not a happy moment, though it is often accompanied by a sense of relief or release.

Of greatest importance to these decisions is the availability of adequate information and accurate identification of alternatives. Physician judgment and physician communications are key to good decisionmaking, though other parties to the process, including other health professionals and family members and friends, can be either helpful or hindering.

Prognosis, a judgment about what the future is likely to hold both with continued treatment and without it, is the sort of judgment that physicians are uniquely trained to make. Patients, family members and even other health professionals are dependent upon the physicians to make these judgments and to communicate them. Failure to do so is not uncommon and is the proximate cause of much disordered decisionmaking and much unnecessary suffering.

When Elizabeth Kubler-Ross began her ground-breaking research a generation ago, the first thing she learned was that few of her physician colleagues at a large public hospital acknowledged having any dying patients. Thanks to Dr. Kubler-Ross and many others, the incidence of professional denial is surely lower today. However, it is still common to find patients whose acknowledgment that they have come to the end of their lives is achieved without any direct help from their medical advisor. In every hospital there are nurses and senior residents who can identify a handful of attending physicians who seem never to recognize impending death until it is unmistakable to even untrained observers. Here, the failure to provide adequate information is not a matter of factual inaccuracy, but flawed medical judgment.

It is also not uncommon for physicians and other professionals to acknowledge among themselves that a patient is irretrievably dying, but not to communicate that effectively to the patient or family. Few of us like to be bearers of bad news; but if that is part of one's job, then a failure to effectively communicate it is a failure of duty and a subtle form of the ancient physicianly sin of abandonment. Other members of the health care team may be slow to compensate for the physician's failure. Nurses, consulting physicians, social workers, respiratory therapists, and other professionals are often reluctant to assume a function often thought to be, and sometimes jealously guarded as, the exclusive province of the attending physician.

Put most plainly, many patients and families cannot and do not make good and timely decisions in large part because they are not told the truth and are either given, or allowed to persist in, false hopes for recovery or survival. Whether because of ignorance, a lack of nerve or a powerful need to avoid, some physicians all of the time and many physicians some of the time seem unable to effectively communicate to their patients or their patients' families that death is near. The consequences for sound health care decisions are serious. Appropriate choices about when to switch from cure care to comfort care depend absolutely upon medical judgments about what it is reasonable to expect.

More common than the failure to make or communicate the medical determination that a patient is entering the final stages of his disease process is the failure to appropriately identify alternatives. The main culprits here are attitudes and habits of thought: the modern notion of the physician as one who "fights" disease and our liberal faith that there is a potential technological solution for every problem.

Acknowledgment that cure-oriented treatment may no longer be appropriate is often presented as though it means the end of therapy. "There's nothing more we can do," is a familiar refrain. The alternative to more chemotherapy or other life-prolonging intervention is seen as "giving up." This defeatist language both reflects and creates negativity and hopelessness. It suggests abandonment and, because of relentless specialization, may indeed signal a change to a completely new set of professional caregivers.

Dr. Patricia Murphy, a nurse specializing in bereavement and clinical ethics, has proposed a more positive and accurate way to frame the ethical question about foregoing cure-oriented treatment. The core idea is to characterize the choice as between two vigorous and ongoing forms of therapy, rather than seeing one choice as doing nothing or giving up. To counter the passivity and defeatism of the common perception, Dr. Murphy has coined the acronym "ACT," or Aggressive Comfort Treatment, as a way to characterize the alternative to aggressive efforts to reverse or arrest the disease process.

ACT is not merely a way to put a positive spin on an otherwise depressing decision point. It actually helps correct a false impression that palliative care is "nothing" and the misleading notion that medicine has no concern for the alleviation of pain or enhanced quality of life.

It is true that palliative care has been overshadowed by curative medicine for the past fifty years. Physicians and nurses do a notoriously poor job of pain control at the end of life, according to many observers and several important national studies. The negative language typically used to characterize the option of shifting treatment to comfort-oriented goals has affected the attitudes and shriveled the competencies of health care professionals. It has undoubtedly influenced patients, families and professionals to pursue life-prolonging treatment long after they might otherwise have switched to therapies that maximize quality of life.

Language is powerful. It shapes perceptions and conditions choices. Perhaps ACT will prove to be a semantic force for the rehabilitation of palliative care as an essential medical competency. In the meantime, it suggests a way to help patients, families and professionals to avoid guilt-driven and misbegotten pursuit of elusive goals because they did not want to "give up."

Do-Not-Resuscitate and Do-Not-Hospitalize Orders. In hospitals, decisions to forego cardiopulmonary resuscitation (CPR) are the most frequently made decisions with regards to withholding potentially life-sustaining treatment. Outside hospitals, the most frequent such decision is probably the conceptually related decision not to send a dying patient to the hospital when that patient shows signs of impending cardiopulmonary failure. Such decisions are properly recorded in medical orders entered into the patient's record after agreement by the patient or patient surrogate that CPR and its usual intensive-care aftermath would not be of net benefit.

Do-Not-Resuscitate (DNR) orders and Do-Not-Hospitalize (DNH) orders are appropriate for those patients who are: dying; permanently unconscious or seriously demented; in a condition that is both very burdensome and irreversible; or unlikely to survive in other than an intensive care environment. It should be obvious that sound decisions about DNR or DNH orders are dependent upon the sort of prognostic judgments discussed at length in the preceding section. Patients or patient surrogates depend upon physicians to make and communicate these prognostic judgments upon which they can then form an opinion about whether CPR and its aftermath is "worth it."

Patients and families need to know about the probabilities of success for CPR relative to the patient's condition. Laypeople are commonly shocked to learn that the success rate (measured in survival to discharge) of many of the hospitalized patients most likely to receive CPR is as low as one or two percent. Physicians who simply ask, "Do you want us to try to restart her heart if it stops?" are likely to get an answer that is unsound by virtue of its being grossly uninformed or misinformed. The remedy is clear. Patients (and, more often, families) need to be told about the probability of success.

Physicians or other professionals who engage in these decision-making dialogues can (and, arguably, should) also recommend or advise, rather than merely dispassionately ask. There is something ironic about a physician who has always offered recommendations at each treatment decision point until death is in view, and then suddenly has only questions and no more advice. This subtle behavioral shift suggests that the physician is disengaging at precisely the point at which a grieving patient or family most needs the constancy of a trusted and familiar medical advisor.

The choice about DNR is often presented as though it were a choice between life and death. It is ordinarily not really that at all. DNR should be more accurately and realistically seen as a choice between two kinds of death. Health professionals (or perceptive non-professionals) should frame the DNR decision for grieving family members in terms like this:

"Your dad has come close to the end of his life. While it is impossible to predict how long he might manage to live, we can say with considerable confidence that he will not get significantly better and that his heart will fail—probably sooner than later. You all understand that, do you not?

"OK, since we are agreed that your dad's death is close, I think the goal of care from this point forward should be to do everything we can to assure his comfort and to enhance his chances to enjoy whatever life remains. I think we're all committed to that goal. Right?

"Now, when his heart does finally give out, it would be technically feasible to try CPR. I don't think we should do that. The chances of it working are practically nil and I'd rather see you all gathered at his bedside, speaking soothing words to him and each other and putting a cool washcloth on his forehead and telling him you love him. *That's* good care for him when his poor old heart finally gives out. CPR won't really help and doing it will mean that you can't do what we know *will* help. What do *you* think about this?"

This kind of decisional guidance is notable, not only for its accurate information about the probabilities of successful CPR and for the helpful advice offered by the physician, but for the way in which the alternatives are framed. The choice is not between doing something and doing nothing, but between two differing interventions, one aimed at life extension and one aimed at life enhancement. If the reframing were motivated by a desire to sugarcoat and obscure, it would not be a worthy suggestion. Rather, it is justified on the basis of giving this family a more realistic and accurate understanding of the nature and consequences of the decision at hand. Finally, this approach is much more apt to afford the survivors the comfort, support and confidence of a caring, fully engaged professional who shares in the decision with them.

Tube Feeding

The provision of hydration and nutrition through plastic tubing is a technological intervention frequently considered when patients cannot take food or drink by mouth. Tube feeding can be accomplished by way of tubes inserted through the nose and into the stomach (*nasogastric tube* or *NG tube*), or surgically implanted through the abdominal wall into the stomach (*G tube* or *PEG*) or (less commonly) into the small intestine (*J tube*). Also, for shorter periods, nutrients can be delivered through small-bore tubes directly into the bloodstream (*hyperalimentation* or *HAL*).

There is rarely any question about the appropriateness of artificially-delivered hydration and nutrition when the intervention is employed as a bridging maneuver to support the patient over a critical period until relative health is restored. However, questions may and often do arise when the incapacity to take oral feedings is a feature of a condition from which the patient is not expected to recover. Examples include:

- a 60-year-old woman who has suffered a massive stroke from which recovery is thought to be remote;
- a 75-year-old man with far-advanced Alzheimer's Disease who does not eat enough to maintain good nutrition;
- an 88-year-old woman with congestive heart failure which confines her to her bed and bedside chair and who, despite "having her full mental faculties," has little appetite and wishes that her daughter would just stop constantly pressing her to eat.

In each of these cases, someone among the professional or family caretakers will suggest—and perhaps passionately insist upon—artificial hydration and nutrition. In each case, someone else will almost surely wonder aloud whether tube feeding is appropriate or vigorously argue that it is not. The symbolism of food and drink and the emotionally loaded associations of food with caring, nurturing, comfort and family duties will almost surely play a role in decision-making about the care of these patients.

Very careful attention to the way key words and concepts are employed would be required as the family members of each of these patients think and talk about whether to institute, withhold or withdraw tube feeding. They will almost surely be vulnerable to emotional and intellectual manipulation. Someone—perhaps, regrettably, a nurse or physician or clergy person—may say to them, "you wouldn't want your mother to starve, would you?"

Sound decisions in such cases require that great care be taken to preserve important distinctions and remain clear-headed. For example, while "starvation" may describe what would happen in the body of an unconscious patient, there would be no subjective experience of deprivation in that patient. An emotionally laden statement such as "your mother will starve" conjures up images of concentration camp victims whose experience is totally unlike that of a profoundly brain-damaged, permanently vegetative stroke victim.

Dying patients who are alert, like the 88-year-old woman with end-stage heart disease, typically lose interest in food, a kind of anorexia of the dying. There is no evidence that they suffer. In any case, if such patients become hungry or thirsty, they can simply ask for or accept food and drink.

In all these instances, allusions to "starvation" are misleading. Such language by well-meaning people turns out to arise from ideological agendas or careless assumptions. It is not helpful for emotionally vulnerable family members trying to discern the right thing to do in confusing circumstances.

Careful attempts to distinguish between "feeding" and mechanically-mediated nutritional support are important to clear thinking. There is a world of difference between patiently offering Grandma a few spoonfuls of applesauce or Ensure pudding and pumping a pharmaceutically prepared preparation directly into her stomach through a length of plastic tubing. A whole lot more than calories and minerals is being conveyed through assisted spoon-feeding. Offering that spoonful is what we have been doing for our young, our old and our sick since time began. That, not tube feeding, is what is always obligatory.

One of the often overlooked consequences of resorting to tube feeding is that we stop or reduce the symbolically and interpersonally rich "nourishment" that accompanies assisted feeding. To speak carelessly, or rhetorically, of tube feeding as if it were the same thing as a daughter lovingly helping her dying mother sip some broth or ginger ale is inaccurate and unhelpful. It does not lead to sound decisionmaking, especially by those who are making choices in the context of anticipatory grief.

Summary

Family members, friends and health care professionals who share responsibility for health care decisions with or on behalf of persons during a prolonged illness make those decisions in the midst of their grieving. Grief can complicate the decisionmaking; less-than-optimal decisionmaking can complicate the grieving.

Both as a way to assure sounder decisions and as a way to avoid unnecessary complications of grief, those who would support others through such hard times would do well to pay attention to the characteristics of sound decisionmaking. In this chapter, we have identified some marks of good ethical thinking:

- adequate information
- appropriate identification of alternatives
- identification of decisionmakers
- identification of stakeholders
- tolerance as affirmative respect
- clarity about key terms and concepts

Finally, we have looked at several specific decisions or ethical dilemmas commonly faced in the course of prolonged fatal illnesses. In the context of these situations, we have identified some unhelpful behaviors and suggested strategies that support quality decisionmaking.

Hospice Care and Its Effect on the Grieving Process

5

William Lamers, Jr., M.D.

Introduction

This chapter will deal with these three areas:

- How are new illnesses (HIV/AIDS and Alzheimer's) challenging the concepts of hospice care?
- How has hospice care affected the grieving process?
- How is hospice likely to affect the grieving process in the future?

Historical Perspective

In the early 1970s, persons who developed cancer and were not cured by aggressive therapies were almost always hospitalized during the final stages of life, separated from their home and their loved ones. Management of pain and symptoms was rudimentary and often inadequate. Home care during the final stages of cancer was uncommon for a variety of reasons: poor symptom management frequently precluded care at home; most home health agencies focused their efforts on providing care to patients who could be rehabilitated following illness or injury; physicians rarely made house calls; the rise of third-party reimbursement mandated standardized, observable, institutional care; changed family structure reduced the availability of care by women in the family; and most families could not afford the cost of private duty nursing in the home. Hospice as we know it in the United States arose out of this challenging milieu (Lamers, 1990). As the cost of hospital care increased, patients who were deemed unable to benefit from further stay were transferred to a lower level of care. Some went home; others went to nursing homes. Government and private insurers sought to conserve resources by limiting physician visits to nursing-home patients. Resources were increasingly diverted to high-technology procedures performed in the acute care setting. By default, the needs of dying persons and their families were given a low priority.

Early Hospice Development

The earliest development of hospice care in the United States was unregulated and not reimbursed. Most early hospice patients had a diagnosis of cancer; most spent the majority of their final weeks or months in their own homes. Care was provided by a combination of family, friends and volunteers under the direction of the hospice interdisciplinary team. The initial handful of hospice programs in this country came together in the mid-1970s to develop a national organization which, among others things, defined and described the essential elements of hospice care. The description of hospice and standards of care developed by the National Hospice Organization provided the larger health care system and potential reimbursement mechanisms with a clear description of how hospice differed from conventional aggressive care or routine home care (National Hospice Organization, 1986).

Among other things, the description of hospice and hospice standards drew attention to the psychosocial and spiritual needs of dying persons and their families. This was a unique declaration, for no other area of health care formally addressed the full dimension of the person. The 'Standards' of the National Hospice Organization in the United States thus paralleled the formulation of 'Assumptions and Principles of Terminal Care' developed by the International Work Group on Death, Dying and Bereavement (IWG, 1977).

Because early hospice programs in the United States believed firmly in the multi-dimensional, indivisible complexity of the 'person,' it was inevitable that early descriptions of hospice included the patient and family together as the 'unit of care.' Early hospice developers saw the need to attend to the spiritual dimensions of the patient, not in a proselytizing way, but as a way of emphasizing that dying persons and their families usually have spiritual beliefs or a religious heritage which play a central role in easing the stress of loss and grief.

Early hospice developers also believed that survivors should have access to support during bereavement. The Standards Committee of the National Hospice Organization mandated that hospice programs provide support for bereaved persons for at least one year following the death of the identified patient. This mandate contrasted with the lack of attention to needs of bereaved persons in the rest of the health care field.

The late 1970s and early 1980s saw an increase in the number of hospice programs across the United States. The National Hospice Organization eventually approached the Joint Commission on Accreditation of Healthcare Organizations (JCAHO) and together they developed the basis for hospice program accreditation. Accreditation served to advance the inclusion of hospice services within the Medicare Benefit. Of interest here is that both JCAHO and Medicare acknowledged the importance of the social, psychological and spiritual elements of hospice care. Through inclusion of these elements, the basic hospice concepts were defined to include not just attention to the physical needs of patients but also to the social, psychological, spiritual and bereavement needs of patient and family. Hospice was therefore clearly distinguished from traditional home care and was identified as more than mere palliation or relief of symptoms of dying persons.

With this as background, we can look at the objectives for this chapter. Each question (How are new illnesses challenging the concepts of hospice care? How has hospice care affected the grieving process? How is hospice likely to affect the grieving process in the future?) will be examined in some detail. But before proceeding it is important to note that it is difficult to generalize about hospice because:

• There is no such thing as a typical hospice patient
• There is no such thing as a typical course of final illness

- There is no such thing as a typical hospice family
- There is no such thing as a typical hospice program
- There is no such thing as a typical bereavement program.

How are New Illnesses (HIV/AIDS and Alzheimer's) Challenging the Concepts of Hospice Care?

Hospice is a program of care provided to terminally ill persons by an interdisciplinary team with emphasis on relief of distressing symptoms, provision of care in the home, inclusion of the patient and the family in the 'unit of care,' availability of bereavement services for at least one year, availability of spiritual care and respect for patient/family lifestyle. Hospice programs attempt to provide optimal relief of symptoms (physical, social, psychological and spiritual) in the patient/family unit. Hospice focuses on the management of pain and other symptoms that often accompany advanced terminal illness. Hospice strives to improve the quality of whatever life remains for the patient and offers support for survivors during bereavement (Stoddard, 1992).

In the mid-70s, the major admitting diagnosis to hospice was advanced, incurable cancer. The recent rise in referrals to hospice of non-cancer diagnoses does not challenge the basic concepts of hospice care. These basic concepts, listed above, are immutable. They do not change regardless of the admitting diagnosis. The economics of hospice reimbursement, however, raises questions about the feasibility of admitting certain patients with non-cancer diagnoses to the Medicare Hospice Benefit.

Are basic hospice concepts challenged by HIV/AIDS and Alzheimer's disease? I do not believe basic concepts of hospice are challenged by the number of patients referred with diagnostic categories other than cancer. The economic well-being of some programs may be challenged. If there is a crisis, it does not concern the integrity or validity of the basic concepts of hospice care. The challenge of new diagnostic categories will bring about some change in the availability of hospice care. Hopefully, hospice services will be available to a broader population and will become better known to the public and physicians.

Although in this chapter we focus primarily on AIDS and Alzheimer's disease, we must also mention chronic obstructive pulmonary disease (COPD), which presents significant prognostic and treatment challenges to hospice caregivers. Persons with advanced COPD often have other interrelated, chronic disease states which complicate the provision of symptomatic relief. Hospice can provide considerable symptomatic relief and emotional support to COPD patients and their families. Symptomatic relief, whether physical, psychological, social, spiritual or some combination, can significantly alter the prognosis, especially if referral is early enough so that the patient/family recieves full therapeutic benefit of the hospice interdisciplinary team. The same is true for persons with AIDS and a number of other non-cancer diagnoses.

At present, hospice faces several challenges regarding the broadening of diagnoses.

Challenge: Can hospice afford to provide excellent care for patients with less certain prognostic futures than is generally now the case?

Concern: The admission of too many patients who survive past an arbitrary time limit jeopardizes economic survival.

Need: Improved prognostic projections for 'new' (to hospice) diagnoses.

Time and severity related reimbursement plans, with higher levels of reimbursement for brief admissions and acute care, lower levels of reimbursement for extended and lower intensity care.

Challenge: Can hospice work with insurers to develop new reimbursement techniques for patients whose symptom management (palliation) requires costly interventions for which hospice is currently not reimbursed?

Concern: Clarification of extent and cost of palliative therapies prior to admission.

Need: Research into the risks and benefits of various therapies for palliation of symptoms in diagnoses new to
hospice.

Challenge: Can hospice work with other health and regulatory
agencies to provide economic application of hospice
concepts and philosophy to patients with indeterminate prognosis?

Concern: Palliative care extends survival past arbitrary time
limits.

Need: Research to determine life extension through palliation.
Cost-effectiveness of palliation vs. traditional care.

Challenge: Can hospice provide the general population and a
highly competitive health care system with an awareness of the values inherent in palliative care once
aggressive care is no longer appropriate?

Concern: After twenty years, hospice still provides care to a
minority of dying persons in the United States.

Need: Hospice education in medical schools and other
professional health care training.
Research establishing the cost-effectiveness of hospice
care.
Public education regarding the advantages of hospice
care.

Challenge: In the increasingly competitive health care market,
funding for hospice care will likely diminish rather
than increase.

Concern: To remain competitive, some hospice programs may
compromise the quality and availability of essential
hospice services including psychosocial services,
bereavement, and spiritual support.

Need: Ongoing program review by licensing, accreditation,
reimbursing and regulatory agencies.

No doubt there are other important concerns. These, however, are some of the major ones that will affect the availability of hospice services in the short term. Concerns for hospice viability in the future include the above challenges plus the overriding challenge of educating the public and health care providers to the benefits of hospice care.

There is reason for concern over the sudden interest in hospice development. Many persons new to hospice do not understand the fundamental principles and practices of palliative care. They view hospice as simply a better-reimbursed variant of home care and therefore pay only lip service to the inclusion of necessary psychosocial care, spiritual care and bereavement support.

The admission of increasing numbers of patients with extended or indeterminate prognoses present not only economic but ethical challenges as well. Advanced AIDS has a less predictable prognosis than cancer, the disease upon which most basic hospice concepts were developed. Should the patient outlive the admitting estimated prognosis, the hospice may be liable for considerable unanticipated expense. This may result in certain hospice programs becoming unwilling to accept persons with a diagnosis of HIV/AIDS. In addition, palliative treatment of some of the common complications of HIV/AIDS can be very costly. Medications required to suppress or modify some of the common side effects of infections associated with immuno-suppression can cost thousands of dollars per month more than the hospice program receives for providing care.

There is no simple 'yes' or 'no' answer to the question of whether or not HIV/AIDS challenges the application of hospice concepts. Most would agree that the lessons learned in the pre-AIDS hospice era proved helpful when communities began to deal with increasing numbers of young persons with rapidly advancing symptoms, including neuro-psychological symptoms (dementia) that are only rarely seen in advanced cancer. The challenge to hospice consisted primarily of a tremendous need for hospice services by a younger age group that often lacked health insurance, lacked traditional family structure, and usually lacked adequate economic resources for prolonged care.

In the first wave of AIDS patients to reach hospice, physicians and nurses were challenged to provide symptom control. The next generation of AIDS patients began to experience not only improved symptom control, but the beginnings of aggressive therapies directed at control of inter-current infections resultant from impaired immune status. This brought about a gradual lengthening of the prognosis for patients who several years earlier would have doubtless experienced shorter periods of survival. The challenge to hospice programs and the entire heath care system was how to pay for the enormous costs associated with palliative symptom management in advanced AIDS at the same time as the financial base for medical research was being pressured to find a cure for the disease.

It is often difficult to establish an accurate prognosis for persons with advanced Alzheimer's disease. NHO has recently developed guidelines for determining the appropriateness of persons with non-cancer diagnoses for admission to hospice programs (National Hospice Organization, 1996). Providing symptomatic relief to persons with HIV/AIDS and Alzheimer's disease commonly extends life as the quality of life improves. Providing symptomatic relief to patients with advanced congestive heart failure provides a model for the dilemma of providing palliative care to patients with non-cancer diagnoses. Relief of recurrent or chronic symptoms of congestive heart failure provides improved quality of life and may extend life beyond six months and leave the hospice program with an unacceptable economic liability.

Before the Medicare Hospice Benefit there was no need to establish an admission prognosis of less than six months. The six-month prognosis was included to limit Medicare's economic liability for the hospice benefit. For patients with advanced cancer who had completed relevant aggressive therapies, this temporal limitation was quite appropriate. There was an occasional exception. But in general it provided hospice programs with a comfortable time frame for providing hospice care.

It is only in the past ten years that appreciable numbers of patients with AIDS have been referred to certain hospice programs. Christakis and Escarce report that in 1990 less than twenty percent of hospice referrals in five major states carried a non-cancer diagnosis

(Christakis and Escarce, 1996). It is only in the last five years that hospice programs have begun to regularly accept referrals of patients with Alzheimer's disease. The broadening of hospice care to include patients with diseases other than cancer fulfills the hope that hospice principles and practices would find wider application. The extension into new diagnostic categories has not been without some concerns, however.

- Non-cancer prognosis is less accurate than the prognosis for patients with cancer. Therefore, it is more difficult to predict which patients will fit within the six-month criterion set by Medicare and most reimbursement entities.
- If too many patients with extended prognosis are admitted to hospice, there is a possibility that the quality of care will be diminished to a point that there is virtually no difference between hospice care and conventional care.
- As more patients with non-cancer diagnoses are admitted to hospice programs, the potential for non-compliance with regulations increases, bringing with it the potential that admission and retention criteria will become more restrictive and more rigidly enforced.
- As more patients with less determinate prognoses are admitted to hospice care, more health care dollars will be appropriated to hospice care. This, in turn, will draw entrepreneurs to develop programs simply to provide minimal hospice care at the risk of jeopardizing the original concept of hospice care.
- For patients with a non-cancer diagnosis, there is a fine line between symptom management and appropriate treatment leading to life-extension. For patients enrolled in hospice care, this can cause combined economic and ethical dilemmas not usually perceived prior to entry into the hospice program. On the one hand, the hospice will want to relieve symptoms secondary to the admitting diagnosis. At the same time, symptom relief may extend life so that the patient is technically ineligible (because of lack of symptoms) but is maintained on hospice enrollment past the usual period of eligibility. Further, the hospice, patient and family are often divided over the delay or withholding of treatments

and therapies aimed at symptom relief. The patient and family may have individually or collectively agreed that now is the time to forego all further treatments. If the hospice persists in advocating or providing symptom relief, the family, the patient and perhaps even the referring physician may feel cause to disagree with the hospice. The opposite situation may also prevail in which the hospice feels a need to dissuade the patient and/or the family and attending physician from what appears to be a reluctance to "let nature take its course."

Nonetheless, Medicare cannot deny coverage to a patient who, because of symptomatic treatment, survives longer than the arbitrary six-month period. The major consideration during Medicare review is, "How long can the patient remain stable and still qualify for the Medicare Hospice Benefit?" As long as the patient meets the NHO 'Guidelines' and the hospice believes the prognosis is less than six months, the patient can continue to receive the Medicare Hospice Benefit. Medicare suggests hospice programs carefully scrutinize any patient who has not experienced measurable decline for two consecutive months.

Another approach is to differentiate between therapies providing symptomatic relief which incidentally prolong life and those non-curative yet also life-extending therapies (e.g., protease inhibitors for AIDS). Hospice generally considers the latter type of treatments outside the scope of palliative care. Some would suggest that patients obtain coverage for such 'outside' therapies from sources other than hospice.

These are but a few things to keep in mind when considering how new diagnostic categories are accepted into hospice. The major new diagnostic categories considered for admission into hospice programs include HIV/AIDS, Alzheimer's disease (dementia), renal (kidney) disease, liver disease, lung disease, amyotrophic lateral sclerosis (ALS or Lou Gehrig's disease) and patients with stroke (cerebro-vascular accident) and coma. Is it proper to say that the addition of new disease categories challenges the concept of hospice care? No—the addition of these categories challenges the application of these principles to non-cancer diagnoses. Of course, the entry of these diagnostic categories extends the potential of hospice care to a greater number of patients, but at the price of hospice programs developing considerable non-reimbursable economic liability. The transition of hospice from a cancer-centered focus to include a broader range of diagnostic categories presents a challenge to the *application* of basic hospice concepts. It forces a necessary re-evaluation of hospice, a re-examination of the values inherent in the hospice concept, an assertion that the larger health care system must begin to consider the total person together with the family. This has not previously been the case.

Moreover, these challenges to the hospice concept are raised within an economic and regulatory framework that is itself in the midst of serious turmoil. If, in the process of helping hospice survive, basic hospice concepts are compromised, there is little likelihood that they will be resurrected in the foreseeable future. This is a critical time. Can hospice survive current challenges? I believe it can. Hospice has proven its value in work with many thousands of families in urban communities and rural areas all over America. Hospice proponents must overcome inertia in the health care field that automatically defaults referrals of dying patients to further aggressive care or to a non-palliative, minimal care environment.

How Has Hospice Care Affected the Grieving Process?

The self-help movement during the 1970s witnessed the establishment of a number of bereavement support programs, some with extensive nationwide links. There was usually a common theme to these groups, whether it was a response to the death of a child (Compassionate Friends), death of a child from cancer (Candlelighters), death of a husband (Widow-to-Widow), and other programs for survivors who have lost a loved one to murder, suicide or sudden death. Most of these groups operated on a voluntary basis at low, if any, cost to the participants. Psychosocial workers know of the value of such programs and routinely refer bereaved persons to them for the valued support they can receive.

As hospice programs arose in the United States, there was strong feeling among the early developers that bereavement support should be an integral part of every hospice program. Formal support for survivors during bereavement was included in the first and subsequent 'Standards' documents of the National Hospice Organization. As NHO sought accreditation as the basis for later reimbursement, bereavement support was included as an essential element of hospice care. This belief in the value of bereavement to the hospice concept later was included in the regulations written to implement the Medicare Hospice Benefit.

Persons participating in effective hospice bereavement support recognize the value of group support, the importance of examining the complicated nature of relationships, and the strength that can derive from dealing with reality in a structured setting. They sense the worth of trusting others who have gone or are going through a comparable experience. They learn the power of emotions related to attachment and loss. They learn that others are there who can help and that support comes not only from group leaders and therapists but from other people with similar problems. The bereavement experience, among other things, teaches bereaved persons to be as benevolent with themselves as they are with others.

Many years ago Erikson said, "Grief, successfully handled, can serve as the focus for new social and psychological growth" (Erikson, personal correspondence). The efforts of hospice bereavement support programs have proved the value of this statement thousands of times. Successful graduates of thousands of hospice bereavement programs have learned to speak about their feelings, to speak openly of the loss they have survived. At the same time they also speak of the value of hospice care, of the value of participating in caregiving and of the fact that it is possible to experience new personal, social and psychological growth out of the depths of the loss of a loved one.

Although reimbursement for bereavement support was not included in the Medicare Hospice Benefit, the mere fact that it was recognized as central to the hospice concept was a large step forward. No other program in health care recognizes the needs of bereaved persons and mandates the availability of extended participation in support programs as an identified benefit. This, in itself, is significant. In this sense, hospice is unique, and the lessons learned from hospice bereavement support programs can be used as a basis for evaluating the implementation of bereavement support to other areas of care. The benefit of unsophisticated, mutual support during bereavement has been amply researched and documented (Raphael, 1977; Connor, 1996).

Hospice has affected the grieving process in a number of other ways:

- Hospice has directed attention to the needs of bereaved persons and developed a variety of models to meet the needs of survivors. *Grief* and *bereavement* are words more commonly heard in discussions than before the advent of hospice care.
- Hospice has championed the use of mutual support groups as developed by a number of other organizations (e.g., Candlelighters, Widow-to Widow programs).
- Hospice has supported the return of bereavement program graduates to become hospice program volunteers. The countless hours of service provided by persons helped through hospice bereavement programs further enriches the care available to new patients and families.
- Hospice has drawn attention to the needs of all family members during bereavement. The needs of children and even grandchildren are not neglected, as was generally the case prior to the advent of hospice.
- Through the publication of articles on bereavement care in both lay and professional journals, hospice has helped remove some of the taboos once associated with dying and death.
- Hospice bereavement programs have developed expertise in dealing with the bereavement needs of persons of different social, ethnic and spiritual backgrounds.
- Hospice programs have shown that support for newly bereaved persons can result in reduced health care costs when compared to a control group that did not receive such support.

Although hospice has been under development in the United States for over twenty years it has still not reached an optimal level of penetration. Too many people with chronic, incurable disease are not referred to hospice. Many physicians do not know about hospice, do not understand the hospice philosophy or are reluctant to share the care of dying patients with a team that purports to possess knowledge about an area of care once the sacred domain of physicians.

The rise of managed care has spurred competition for patients. The physician with a dwindling caseload, dwindling income or both, is reluctant to refer a patient to a program that appears competitive to the physician. Most physicians do not understand that their continuing involvement is sought by hospices and that they can still bill for many of the patient services they render. Hospice is not the competition many physicians fear it is.

How is Hospice Likely to Affect the Grieving Process in the Future?

The grieving process itself will remain unchanged in the future. But hospice, if it has any influence at all, will enhance the possibility that low-tech, readily available extended bereavement support will become available to bereaved persons outside of the hospice experience.

If hospice programs are going to obtain maximum benefit from bereavement programs in the future, they must learn to implement them wisely and use them effectively. Those who lead bereavement support programs must be properly trained, adequately supervised and supported by the other elements of the program, from administration to patient care. In the early days of hospice development in the United States bereavement support was often seen as "the poor step-child of hospice care." Bereavement support for many programs at the time was a costly add-on, a drain on the budget, a needless burden on an always overworked and underpaid staff. Yet those programs that developed effective bereavement support learned that such a program can provide entry into an otherwise impenetrable professional community. Graduates of hospice bereavement support programs generally become the staunchest proponents of hospice care.

Many of them return later to become superb patient care and administrative volunteers.

The most likely scenario is that increasing numbers of patients will be referred for hospice care, that accreditation and certification will mandate the development of improved bereavement support programs and that, eventually, hospice programs will provide bereavement support services for a nominal fee to survivors referred by managed care organizations. These referrals will stem from the growing recognition that survivors participating in excellent bereavement support require fewer medical services than those not participating in such programs.

Summary

The multi-dimensional (physical, social, psychological, spiritual) needs of dying persons, family and caregivers do not change appreciably regardless of the duration of the dying. With sufficient time and direction in an optimal program, many of these needs can be met and the experience can be beneficial to all concerned. It is reasonable to assume that the expansion of hospice admitting criteria to include patients with non-cancer diagnoses does not challenge basic hospice concepts. It is also clear that the admission of patients who require expensive treatments to maintain their quality of life, plus patients whose prognosis improves as symptoms are relieved, pose a challenge to the application of basic hospice concepts.

Currently, this is especially true of persons with AIDS. Despite the ready availability of hospice programs, relatively few seek hospice care, most likely because of the availability of new combination therapies, including protease inhibitors. Some maintain that AIDS will become a 'chronic disease' requiring successive levels of esoteric and increasingly expensive aggressive therapies. Others suspect that some sort of cure will be discovered, possibly a vaccine, that will curb the transmission of AIDS. A few voice concern that the 'AIDS epidemic' is just beginning and that in a few years this country must deal with new waves of persons with AIDS, including young women who contracted the disease during their teens and twenties.

To insure that hospice survives these challenges, several things are required:

- Closer program monitoring of admission diagnosis and prognosis
- The development of several new levels of hospice care:
  - 'traditional' hospice care for persons with fairly definite short-term prognosis (for example, persons with advanced, incurable cancer);
  - 'long term' hospice care for persons with an indeterminate prognosis who do not require expensive therapies to improve the quality of life during a prolonged period of dying (for example, persons with chronic, incurable neurologic disorders like Alzheimer's Disease and ALS);
  - 'high-tech' hospice care for persons who require expensive therapies to maintain reasonable relief of symptoms in the face of a limited, yet uncertain, prognosis (for example, persons with advanced AIDS).

In addition, it is essential that physicians and the general public receive more information about the availability of hospice services and that physicians, patients and health care administrators become aware of the economic benefits of early, appropriate referral of dying persons to hospice. All too few in the health care community, as well as the general population, know when, where and how to refer a patient to hospice care.

In conclusion, AIDS and Alzheimer's disease as well as other non-cancer diagnoses offer some intriguing yet not insurmountable challenges to implementation of the hospice concept. Perhaps the greatest threat to basic hospice concepts will come from those who do not understand hospice, who still treat only the disease or the symptoms and not the total person.

The Story of Miss Mildred: Her Living and Dying

6

Annette Dula

Introduction

This is the life story of an elderly black woman in the rural south. It is a narrative about Miss Mildred's life and death. Miss Mildred is a composite of elderly black women in the rural southern community where I grew up: they are my mothers, grandmothers, aunts, great aunts, and cousins. They are blood and non-blood relatives. This narrative attempts to link the life, the chronic illnesses, and the death of an black elderly woman.

I am presenting a life story because many health care providers do not know the elderly black woman outside the private office, the emergency room, or the clinic. Since what they know about elderly blacks comes from the "experts," I want to let Miss Mildred speak for herself. You will hear how she thinks about her illnesses, her folk health beliefs, her health care providers, her thoughts on life-sustaining therapies and advance directives, and her approaching death.

It is the responsibility of health practitioners to educate patients about advance directives; but it is equally, and perhaps even more important, to educate elderly blacks so that they themselves can participate in managing and controlling their illnesses, thereby improv-

---

Note: Adapted from an earlier work by the author, originally published as Dula, Annette. (1994). "The Life and Death of Miss Mildred", *Clinics in Geriatric Medicine* vol. 10, 3:419–430.

ing the current quality of their lives. But before health care providers can effectively educate, they must have a firm grasp of the life challenges that elderly African Americans have faced throughout their lives. To do this they need to enter the world of the elderly black patient, and they must enter that world with caution and respect.

Who Is Miss Mildred?

In the black community, traditionally, the elderly black woman sits on a throne of grace, emanating an aura of dignity. She is respected for her wisdom, admired for her strength, and honored for her contributions to the health and well-being of both the black family and its community. She is a valuable resource and a knowledgeable advisor because of her life experiences. Her presence provides a steadying and calming influence on younger adults. She plays a critical role in imparting values on work, education, religion, and family and community responsibility. She is an upright, upstanding member of the community; her very presence has served as a buttress against racism and discrimination.

The elderly black woman is never referred to by her first name; she is either Miss Mildred by non-family members (regardless of marital status, adult or elderly black women in the south are called "Miss"); Sister Mildred by her age peers and church ladies; or Aint Mildred by her dozens of younger relatives (Aint is a synonym for Aunt used extensively in some southern communities). She may be called Big Mama by her grandchildren, her great grandchildren, and other blood and non-blood relatives that she has raised and cared for over the years.

Her beautiful flower garden with the snapdragons, zinnias, and azaleas is the talk of the neighborhood. She still cans or "puts up" apples, blackberries, peaches, and tomatoes—all harvested from her own garden with her own hands. At church fetes, members line up to make sure that they get some of Sister Mildred's famous fried chicken and deep-dish peach cobbler.

She is somewhat overweight, but no one in the community would have the nerve to call her fat. One of her church Sisters might dare to say,

— You looking right healthy, Sister Mildred. Life must be treating you pretty good.

Sister Mildred will piously, yet playfully, reply,

— Yes Sister, the Lord's been right good to me. I can't complain. If he calls me tomorra, I'm ready to go.

And under her breath, she might be heard to indignantly mumble:

— Don't you be getting all se-ditty and uppity on me, Tillie Mae. I knowed you before you became a Christian—when you wasn't nothing but a old fast gal, giving your life to the devil.

Miss Mildred's Spirituality

Elderly black women have a very strong faith; they believe in the Lord with all their hearts. They may show it inside or outside the church. As active church participants, they sing in the choir, teach Sunday School, or head a missionary group. Elderly black women occupy a most respected role as elders of the church, and some loudly extol the glory and the grace of God through shouting. They have given to the church all their lives, and when they become sick the church gives back to them. The church provides some material support in hard economic times or in sickness. But most of all, it provides spiritual sustenance. Indeed, the older they get, the more religious elderly black women often become. A friend of mine recently said to me,

— Chile, every time I go home, Mama done got more religious than she was the last time I was home.

There's another group of elderly black women who don't spend so much time in the church, perhaps because of poor health, employment requirements, or lack of transportation. But their faith is just as strong. They pray and read the Bible frequently, listen to religious radio, and watch religious TV. They have been faithful supporters of evangelical ministers for a good number of years. Even if they do not attend church services regularly, they do manage to attend the bigger and more famous of the traveling church revivals and camp meetings.

They contribute financially to the church, even though their income is meager. Although Sister Mildred may have little, she will share her food and visit with the infirm and others doing less well than she. As she puts it,

— I ain't got much, but the Good Lord done said that we got to help them that needs help. We got to give food to the hungry, visit the old folks and the lonely folks, and minister to the sick. Don't matter what color they is neither. We're all God's children.

Miss Mildred's Work

Outside the black community, there is another portrait of the elderly black woman where she is often seen just as a poor old black auntie or as an uneducated domineering matriarch. If her health is not doing too poorly, she may still be a service worker in a private white home or business.

She may not speak "standard" English very well and most likely she has not received formal education beyond the eighth grade. Public school education in the pre-war South revolved around the picking of cotton, the cutting of sugar cane, the harvesting of tobacco, and the explicit and purposeful exclusion of blacks from equal education.

Miss Mildred cooks for the white folks and does a bit of light cleaning. She doesn't work nearly as hard as she did when she first started working for the Smiths. (She's been working for them off and on for the past four decades). Over the years she has worked as hard as any man or woman: she has picked cotton and tobacco; she has nursed white children; she's worked as a domestic worker for several white families; and she's washed and ironed white folks' laundry in her own home.

— I even worked in a textile mill and in a furniture factory back in the 60's, when they first began letting us women work the shifts. That was the time I said I wasn't going to be no maid for white folks no more. But I had to quit both them jobs. Those chemicals and dust made me dizzy and sick to the stomach. So I went back to work for Miss Smith.

Things have changed a lot since she first started working for Miss Smith. In fact, Miss Mildred's white folks treat her pretty decently now, except at holidays. On Thanksgiving and Christmas they expect her to bake 10 cakes and 10 pies and cook enough food for all Miss Smith's relatives that come in for the holidays:

— It ain't so easy for me to do all that cooking nowadays. My bunions hurt me when I have to stand up for a long time. But Miss Smith is pretty good to me. Since I got old, she hired somebody to help with the cleaning. Now she even lets me leave early on holidays with hardly no fuss a'tall. After all these years, it finally come to her mind that I've got to spend some time with my own family and my own children on holidays.

Miss Mildred's Family and Community

Sister Mildred started her own Thanksgiving dinner about a week before the holiday, so all the food was prepared by Thanksgiving day. She cooked candied yams, a 20-pound turkey, two sweet potato pies, 20 pounds of chitlins' cooked with hot peppers, potato salad, a pork roast, some buttermilk biscuits, and collard greens seasoned with ham hocks and fat back.

— I know I ain't supposed to be eating these foods. And I done cut back on them some. These is the foods that make your blood hot, and rich, and thick. That's when you get high blood. High blood is a disease that done killed lots o' us black folks. Now you can cool down and thin the blood if you take a little bit of garlic water, or lemon juice, or vinegar. That's what my herb doctor told me to do. And I believe it works. But you've got to stop eating pork and grease. That's the hard part, 'cause that's what us old folks was raised on. The pork chitlins', and the ears, and the tails was the parts o' the pig that the white folks didn't want.

Miss Mildred invited all of her family to Thanksgiving dinner. They include her two remaining blood sisters and five middle-aged children. Only ten of the grandchildren came to dinner, but twenty great grandchildren showed up at Big Mama's. Uncle Boy was there too. He has no blood family, but the ladies in the community look out for him and make sure he has at least one good hot meal every day.

All the grandchildren and great grandchildren call Sister Mildred "Big Mama." Big Mama and Daddy Joe raised their nine children, two grandchildren and the two Jones kids. The Jones kids' parents lost their lives in the big fire of 1945. They didn't have anyplace to go, so Big Mama took them in. Sister Hominy still lives with Big Mama. Nobody knows where she came from. She just showed up one day and started living with the family. Now she is family. Thirty years later Miss Hominy and Sister Mildred mostly have the big house to themselves.

Although the black family structure is showing signs of stress, it has traditionally been the strongest African-American institution. One function of the black family has been to act as a buffer against the stress of living in a racist society. The African-American family includes nuclear, extended, and augmented family forms. Strong kinship bonds in which relatives and friends support and reinforce each other are based on African heritage and slavery experience. Often there will be a multigenerational family living under the same roof. And it is likely our composite elderly woman will live in a multigenerational family. Some of those members will be relatives and some will not be relatives. But it doesn't matter. They are all considered family.

Miss Mildred Plans for Her Death

Sister Mildred has been feeling poorly lately. In fact, she hasn't felt too good ever since she had that operation two years ago. They took out her gall bladder. If she had had her druthers, she would not have gone back to Miss Smith's. Lord knows she hadn't felt like it. She liked Miss Smith; she was a nice white lady. The other day Sister Mildred told Miss Hominy,

— I'm so tired. I been cleaning up after white folks nigh on sixty years now. But I needs to take care of my burial. So I needs to keep working.

Miss Mildred had thought about retiring but had decided that,

— Us poor colored women can't retire; that's what white folks do. We just keep on working and getting sicker and sicker. And then we die.

— Sister Hominy, at my funeral, I want you to make sure they put some gladiolas on top o' the hearse that carries m' body. I get a little bit o' money from the government, but honey, you know it ain't much. But one thing's for sure! I ain't got to ask nobody for nothing. I been paying $2.00 a week for my burial ever since I turned 50. Soon's I die Ebony Funeral Home's going to put up two thousand dollars for my burial. I done picked out and paid for my tombstone and a little plot o' land over in Freedman Cemetery. Don't want none of the kin folks to have to put me away.

— I been planning for my death a long time. I know the Lord is coming after me soon. And I'm gonna be ready to go. I want to be buried in that pretty white dress my baby granddaughter give me two years ago. I ain't never wore it but twice. I want little Donna— how old is she now? 'Bout 30, I reckon. I want her to sing "I Am Climbing Jacob's Ladder." That sure is a pretty song.

No matter how poor they may be, many elderly black folks have a little burial insurance on the side.

— I still has to pay for some of my medicine and I have to pay for it out o' that little bit o' money that I get from the government and from Miss Smith. I also set a little money aside each month for the herb doctor. But if I don't have the money, she doctors me just the same.

Although Miss Mildred had been working since she was 11 years old, for the most part, none of her employers had contributed to her social security fund. She did receive Supplemental Security Income (SSI) which was pretty meager, but it did help keep the wolf from the door. She didn't quite understand that Medicare and Medicaid business. Medicaid was supposed to be for poor folks and Medicare for old folks. But even with Medicaid and Medicare help, it was still hard for Miss Mildred to pay for all of her health care needs. Still, she thought,

— Things is much better for us elderly since Mama died. Didn't have no Medicare and Medicaid to help the elderly then. But even if things is better for us than they used to be, I don't believe colored folks get the same care that white folks get.

Yes, Sister Mildred has been feeling poorly lately. It was all she could do to drag herself out of bed everyday and do her housework and put in a few hours at Miss Smith's. But she wasn't quite ready to tell the family how lowly she'd been feeling lately. She will go see Dr. McBee. She doesn't think that Doc McBee was helping her much but since Dr. McBee liked her, Sister Mildred humored the doctor a little bit.

— Dr. McBee treats me real good. But she ain't so good at explaining things. She uses these big words and I don't know a bit more what she's talking about. She told me I had a tumor in my lung that was going to kill me. I didn't know she was talking about cancer until one of my grandchildren asked me if it was malignant. (I didn't know what that word meant either.) I don't know why them doctors can't just come on out and use plain language. Sometimes she don't understand things too good neither. One time my hip was hurting me real bad, and she wanted me to tell her what the pain was like. Now the only thing I could think of was that time I fell off the old mule and got kicked in the side. I told the doctor it had hurt so much that I liked to uh' died.
— And that fool doctor, much as I like her, thought I was saying I wanted to kill myself. That's when she asked me if I knew what euthanasia is. First I thought it had something to do with young people: youth-in-Asia. When she told me what euthanasia is, I looked at her like she was crazy. I was kind of surprised that she even brought it up since sometimes black folks can be mighty touchy about white folks trying to get rid of us. Maybe she went to one of them confer-

ences that she's always going to, and they told her to talk to her patients about these things.

— But you know what? Ever since we talked about it, look like every time I turn on the TV, somebody's talking about euthanasia, physician-assisted suicide, and doctors helping kill off old and sick folks. Well, I ain't seen them ask nary a elderly black on none of them TV shows and news programs what they thought about doctors helping old and sick folks die. I believe the Lord will take me away when it's time to go. Ain't nobody going to hurry me along.

— Now, McBee's been talking about an advance directive. I'm kinda confused. I thought about signing that thing. But I didn't know whether they was going to try to kill me by not giving me good doctoring, or keep me alive on them machines, or keep me doped up on them medicines. I just ain't sure. I don't want to be kept alive on no machines. To tell you the truth, I wouldn't put it past them doctors to kill me off anyhow. Well, I don't really think McBee would kill me off, but she ain't the only doctor that tends me. I done told Sister Hominy what I want done if I get to the place that I can't talk for myself. That way the doctors can't play God and decide that I done lived long enough. Them doctors think a pore old colored lady ain't got no sense a'tall.

— Chile, they had Sister Johnny doped up so bad that she didn't know nothing. Lordy, it was pitiful to see her. She couldn't do nothing for herself. If the family hadn't come in and combed her hair and greased her skin, why, she'da looked like nobody cared nothing about her. The nurses tried to do right. But they don't know how to take care of colored people's skin and hair. Sister Johnny woulda just died of pure dee shame if she coulda knowed that she was messing all over herself. And them nurses, honey. If they was busy, they'd just let her lay in her own mess. I do declare, I don't want to be no burden to nobody. But I don't want them to kill me off, neither. I'm afraid if I sign that living will thing, them doctors will use that piece of paper to kill me off.

— My blood has been real high and the medicine that Dr. McBee give me just ain't working. So I been goin' to the herb doctor over in West End and she's been treating my high blood with garlic. I been rubbing my side in alcohol and camphor for that pain that I been having for so long. My sugar's been high too. My eyesight is bad because of the sugar diabetes; I don't read nothing but the Bible and the newspaper these days. McBee is worried that I am going to get glaucoma and go blind. Well, I'm a bit worried about that too. Even if I ain't got long for this world, I want to see it while I'm here.

Miss Mildred has also been "bleeding from down below." She told her granddaughter that it was like having a period again. It sure is a nuisance, particularly since she had thought that her bleeding was all done with. Sister Mildred thinks that if she can just get through Christmas dinner, she will go see Dr. McBee the next day. She knows that Dr. McBee will find time to see her. She always does.

Miss Mildred has made it through Christmas dinner, but just barely. It was obvious to other members of the family that Sister Mildred was not herself. She seemed to be in a lot of pain. And she had to take to the bed a couple of times to rest a bit.

— I'm just tired,

she told the family when they all tried to make her go the emergency room of the hospital.

— I ain't going to no doctor tonight. I just needs me some rest. Besides the doctor can't do me no good. But, I'll go tomorrow if y'all will quit pestering me. All this aggregation is sure to kill me off even if all these other ailments don't.

After a family discussion, they have decided that 16-year-old BettyeLou will stay with her great grandmother and Miss Hominy that night, in case Big Mama decided to go to the hospital.

In her heart of hearts, Miss Mildred does not want to go to the doctor this time. She is afraid that she will be hospitalized, and for Miss Mildred the hospital is a place for old people to go and die. She'd rather die at home. She is getting along in age, though; she'll be 85 years old come Valentine's Day. That's already longer than most black folks live. She knows her time is coming soon and she has no regrets. All in all, she has had a good life. And she is ready. Most of her friends have already gone home to glory. She is tired too, and about ready to go and see her husband Daddy Joe and her own Mama and Papa. She thinks to herself,

— Daddy Joe sure was a good man. He worked real hard for me and the young'uns. But they beat him to death back in 1959. I always told Daddy Joe that his big mouth was going to get him kilt. Them policemen said he had a heart attack in the jail house. Humph! I knows they beat him to death. And there wasn't nothing I could do about it. Yes, I'm tired and I'm ready to move on where there ain't no more sickness, and meanness, and race hatred.

Miss Mildred Begins the Dying Process

Miss Mildred goes back and forth to and from the hospital several times over the next few months. Although her condition has noticeably deteriorated, collapses in cognition have not occurred. She has been approached on several occasions by her physician who requested that she document her treatment preferences through an advance directive. Dr. McBee understands that Miss Hominy is an informal proxy and that informal directives may be just as binding as formal documents. But since Miss Mildred has so many relatives, her caretaker is afraid there will not be family consensus in carrying out Miss Mildred's wishes. Miss Mildred, after careful consultation with Miss Hominy, her siblings, her youngest daughter, and her pastor, finally agrees to document her preferences. She formally designates Miss Hominy as her proxy. She particularly lets it be known that food and water, whether artificially administered or ingested through the mouth, are to be provided under all conditions.

— Food and water ain't medication. I don't care how they give it to you. If you take away food and water from a person, you might as well kill em. I ain't saying that they have to do every blessed thing. I just want them to respect me and give me good care. Why, you'd give even a thirsty dog some water, wouldn't you? I just want the doctors and the nurses and all these young people learning how to be doctors to treat me just as good as they do the white patients. Like the Good Book say, 'Give comfort to all the sick, not just to some o' them.'

It has been a couple of weeks since Miss Mildred signed the advance directive. She is certainly getting weaker and weaker each day, but her mind is still clear. She has spent some time in the intensive care unit, but now she is back on the floor. She wonders whether she has been put back on the floor because they had given up on her. She's heard that they do that sometimes to make room for white patients. But to be fair, she doesn't really think Doc McBee would let them abandon her, just like that. After all, wasn't it Doc McBee who got the hospice people to come over every day when she was home?

Miss Mildred doesn't feel too good within herself about how she is being treated. Since she has come back from intensive care, she feels that the nurses and doctors are just waiting for her to die. They are kind enough; it was just seems that they had already disengaged themselves from her, they don't seem to care anymore whether she is comfortable or not. When she signed that living will, they'd been oh so careful to promise her that she would get good care and comfort.

Miss Mildred has her good days and her bad days. Yesterday, she choked on her phlegm. BettyeLou had cleaned the phlegm from Big Mama's mouth and kept her lips and tongue moistened with a wet cloth. The worst part, though, was when she had to go to the toilet. Usually someone in the family is around to help her. But every now and then she has to depend on the staff. She does not mind using the bedpan if she only has to make water. But it is a matter of self-respect and pride to get up and go to the toilet for a bowel movement. Thank God she can still get to the bathroom, even though she needs a little help. That morning, she'd rung and rung, but no one had come to see about her. That was it! That's when she had decided that she would just tear up that darn advance directive.

One of the nurses finally showed up, cheerily inquiring, "Hi there Hon. How are we doing this morning?" Big Mama, with all the dignity and iciness that she could muster, answered,

— I don't know how *we* are doing, Nurse, but I want you to go and get me that living will that I signed and bring it here to me so that I can tear it up. Maybe then I can get some attention. Ain't nobody paid no attention to me since I signed that thing.

Miss Mildred decides that she wants to spend as much as possible of her remaining time in her own home among friends and family who are honored and happy to take care of her. Dr. McBee makes arrangements for her to be as comfortable as possible. Different hospice workers spend a couple of hours with her every day. Dr. McBee also manages to find time to drop in each day or so, just to check up on her state and to chat with her. (After all, Mildred's been her patient for 25 years.)

The community will prepare itself and the family for her death; they will talk about all the good Miss Mildred has done, the people she has helped, the wise counsel that she has given. They will joke about how she loved to go fishing almost as much as she loved to go to church. The few old friends that are still living will bring her food (which she will pretend to eat) and sit with her for a spell. Neighbors, friends, or family will clean her house; others will make sure she has clean sheets every day. And the younger ones will comb, brush, and braid her hair daily. Friends and family come in and sit up with Miss Mildred all night if it seems necessary. She will never be left alone. When she dies, someone in the community will most likely be with her to help her cross over into the other land.

Conclusion

I have presented the life story of an elderly black woman because her biography is insufficiently appreciated. However, Miss Mildred should not be seen as a stereotype of the elderly black woman. While a great many elderly black women are religious, live in southern states, and are surrounded by family and friends, a sizable portion do not fit that mold. Many do bask in the warmth and love of family, friends, church, and community, but some live alone in dangerous and poor urban neighborhoods without either kin or social, psychological, and spiritual support. There are other portraits, but I have tried to present a picture of one elderly black woman's life, one which is embedded in a matrix of family, religion, and community. It is a profile in which disparities in access, inequalities in health status, and end-of-life discussions cannot be considered apart from historical, social, and economic aspects of the elderly black woman's life.

After the family, religion is the most important institution in the biographies of many elderly black women and is intricately tied to family life. Religious involvement provides not only spiritual succor, but also social life, practical information, and political consciousness.

If she is seventy-five years old, the elderly employed black has probably been working for at least sixty of those years, yet has no accumulated wealth or assets. Furthermore, she is unlikely to be enrolled in supplementary medical insurance or receive social security benefits, and she may have only a vague understanding of the intricacies of Medicare and Medicaid. Small SSI payments do little to ameliorate her poverty. Therefore she may still be employed part-time as a service worker, not because she wants to work, but because she needs to supplement her income.

The elderly black woman understands white middle-class people because she has been the recipient of intimacies that the white mistress would not even tell her best friend. However, because of race, class, and ethnicity barriers, health care practitioners do not know the elderly poor black outside the clinical setting. To morally intervene in the lives of patients, providers need to understand the culture of their patients, including family and community norms. They need to be familiar with the life stories of their patients; for it is through stories that we begin to empathize with others. Stories open our eyes to other people's ethical dilemmas and dramas surrounding life and death. In a health care system in which the providers are mostly white and the sickest people are elderly African Americans, a larger sense of the patient's story will improve the quality of the everyday practice of medicine and the quality of communication with the person who is ill or approaching death. Understanding and appreciating life histories can go a long way to eliminating the distrust of the health care system that many elderly blacks have.

Miss Mildred taught us that the elderly black woman is a proud and independent being. The idea of controlling the circumstances of one's death does not necessarily contradict the image of a self-sufficient elderly black woman. Rather, the difficulty will be in convincing her that health care providers and the larger society are just as committed to improving access to care and reducing health disparities based on race, as they are to getting her to execute an advance directive. Only then will she be convinced that these measures are neither excuses to kill her off by stopping treatment prematurely, nor prolonging her life beyond God's will, but rather simply a tool to protect her rights and preferences.

PART II

Grief, Loss and the Illness Experience

Some of the earlier theories of how individuals cope with dying and death, such as Kubler-Ross (1969), viewed dying as a universal experience evoking common responses. Yet, while dying is universal, each death experience is very different and distinct for the dying person and the survivors, in part because of the uniqueness of the individual. Each person growing up in his or her own culture has developed characteristic ways to cope with any life crisis, including dying, grief and loss.

Individuals die from different diseases and each disease has its unique course, treatment and side effects. Doka's opening chapter emphasized that the nature of the disease not only affects the dying, but often has residual issues for survivors. This section explores that idea further, reviewing the types of grief reactions that may be evoked by three common illnesses—cancer, AIDS, and Alzheimer's.

Hersh begins by exploring cancer, emphasizing the variety of losses people experience as they cope with the disease. Cancer, in many ways, illustrates the individuality of grieving in prolonged loss. Each form of cancer may create its own unique issues for survivors. Facial cancers may cause disfigurement; other types, such as colon cancer, have other factors that generate strong ambivalence. Suffering, too, can vary with each form of cancer. And in each course of an individual's cancer, a different array of decisions will emerge.

Years ago cancer, because it inevitably seemed to lead to painful death, was the most feared and dreaded disease. Now that distinction belongs to AIDS. Corless' chapter explores the grief generated by AIDS. Many AIDS survivors are disenfranchised because their grief is not acknowledged by others. Sometimes this is due to the nature of the illness. To many, AIDS still carries a stigma, branding one a member of a socially-disapproved group. In other cases, the survivor may have a role, such as a lover, that is not acknowledged by others. Corless also notes that many AIDS survivors have to cope with multiple losses. Like Rando, she sees the experience as evoking trauma. Finally, Corless acknowledges the critical role that ritual can have in validating grief.

Alzheimer's offers a third illustration of the unique issues raised by a specific disease. Williams and Moretta describe the multiple losses that occur with this disease, including the eventual isolation from others. Alzheimer's provides an example of "psychosocial" loss— where the persona of the individual is lost long before the body dies.

Cancer, AIDS, and Alzheimer's are just three examples of diseases that generate distinct grief issues. Conditions such as Huntington's Chorea, amyotrophic lateral sclerosis (ALS), multiple sclerosis, muscular dystrophy, or any other disease, all raise unique issues for survivors. The critical question remains, "How does the course of the disease affect the survivors' subsequent grief?"

Death From The Cancers 7

Stephen P. Hersh, M.D.

As with all chronic illness, the onset of cancer intrudes unexpectedly into the lives of the ill person, close family members, and
friends. For those people with access to modern medical treatments,
only 3 or 4 of the 100 forms of cancer lead fairly rapidly (counted in
months) from diagnosis to death. Most of the 10,000,000 people
living with cancer in the United States exist in a chronic state of
vigilance about their health, combined with uncertainty about their
future. For them uncertainty exists in the form of worries not only
about continued health, but about possible death. Worrying about
death is reinforced by the widely-held popular belief in our culture
that equates a cancer diagnosis with a death sentence. Patients and
family find themselves struggling with a series of necessary adjustments. These adjustments include accepting the reality of the diagnosis; understanding and agreeing to treatments recommended;
coping with the treatments as well as their side effects; reengaging in
activities of daily life (family responsibilities, school, and work); and
realizing that death is *not* imminent.

The quality of life of cancer patients is profoundly influenced by
an extraordinary variety of factors. Factors that influence the experience of cancer for patients and family also influence the experience
of death from cancer. These include the age of the patient, the type
of cancer, the treatments and their consequences, the patient's role in
the family system, and social, economic, and geographic factors. Death

occurs within the context of these life variables, which color the objective realities of the experience, as well as emotions associated with the death. How these factors interact with each other, as well as how they are responded to, determine the quality of the illness experience for each cancer patient and each family; and they affect the survivors' eventual grief.

One of the most common factors is pain. Over time, pain presents itself as a problem for at least 70% of cancer patients. Depending on the duration, extent, intensity, location and treatments offered, pain can either be an unpleasant but manageable part of the cancer experience, or it can be one that produces fatigue, irritability, anger, depression and hopelessness, not only in the patient but also for their most intimate family and friends.

Disfigurement can cause difficulty in the cancer experience. Visible disfigurements range from total body hair loss to limb amputations to colostomies and urostomies, to genital and breast amputations, to skin changes from radiation, to neck and jaw and facial deformities secondary to surgeries. Some disfigurements are more subtle. The lifestyle disruption of chronic fatigue challenges many patients because of its invisibility. It could be considered an invisible form of disfigurement. The burden of embarrassment, feelings of shame, and desires to hide, as they touch on personal, intrafamilial and community self-image, can be extraordinary.

Over the course of living with cancer, not only is the patient's self image challenged, but the patient's family and social roles are frequently modified. Careers may be altered. For children, child development milestones and school participation are changed. Fatigue, recovery from surgery and radiation, toxicity from drugs (including antibiotics and pain medicine) may all alter thinking ability, dampening the sharpness, rapidity, and productivity of the thought processes.

Later in the course of the illness, patients and family members may experience the *Lazarus Syndrome*—he who rose from the dead. Although first described with reference to children with cancer who experience reversals of their dying process when at death's door, the Lazarus Syndrome can be experienced by adults, too. A person may be failing; the patient and family accommodate to this failing and prepare for death, perhaps even to the point of making funeral arrangements. Then, unexpectedly, the ill person's health improves and the individual finds himself or herself discharged from the hospital or hospice. Experiences like these are emotionally wrenching, especially for family members. All are challenged by the sudden need to shift expectations and accommodations. Family members find themselves struggling, often in secret, with wishing that the person had actually died and that the trial of participating in illness and dying was finally completed. Survivors react to these thoughts with feelings of guilt about having had such thoughts in the first place; rarely do individuals confess to these secret thoughts. They often, therefore, go on suffering in silence about having "unforgiveable" thoughts unless they are fortunate enough to participate in a peer group or some other form of support.

The family members of cancer patients experience many forms of grief. They experience grief over the fact of the illness itself. They grieve over the physical and psychological challenges that they see in their loved one: for example, the dramatic diminution of energy as well as the different forms of possible physical disfigurement from weight loss and decreased muscle mass to loss of hair and limbs and other body parts. Certainly the loss of weight and muscle mass itself, as well as the diminution of energy, is universal to the cancer odyssey. Over time, as with all unhappy things, when these changes become constant, familiar realities, an accommodation occurs. Part of the accommodation is really a numbness to the feelings of grief and loss experienced by patient and family members and close friends. The numbness and getting used to the pain of the grief as well as the grief itself are all forms of coping. Such coping allows the involved individuals to persevere in their lives as best they can.

Once a person, be they child or adult, has died from cancer there is a double reality for the survivors. Survivors are definitely relieved that the suffering of their loved one and the added stress of their own lives by that suffering is over. They are simultaneously deeply saddened by the permanence of the physical separation from the deceased loved one.

During the first few weeks after the death of someone who had a prolonged experience with cancer, survivors are left with feelings of relief, numbness, and a vague sense of disbelief that the odyssey is finally completed. The numbness to the feelings of sadness comes and goes, but is rather predominant during the first two to three months after death. That numbness and feeling of distance from memories of the dying process and death itself begin to lift during a second phase from three to six to 14 months. During that phase there occur an increasing number of moments when feelings of grief and a sense of loss are consciously no longer with the person. Such episodes are interspersed with sometimes crashingly powerful feelings and memories associated with the dying loved one and death. These episodes astonish those experiencing them by their intensity as well as their capacity to occur at unexpected moments. Closest friends and family members actually discover that they have some dimensions of a Posttraumatic Stress Syndrome experience: they may suddenly see, or sometimes hear or smell, something that evokes images and memories of their ill, dying, and deceased loved one. These memories can come up spontaneously during the daytime or during dreams at night. During the daytime they may be stimulated by any kind of sensory experience which accesses a trigger memory— a sound similar to a respirator, a smell similar to a hospice or a hospital smell, an image or color similar to an image or color experienced with the dying person. Daytime events can trigger nighttime recall and memories. These recollections which intrude are always associated with feelings of quiet, yet deep, sadness.

Survivors may struggle with memories, going through a prolonged process of recall, reintegration, and redigestion of the person and all the events of the illness experience. Such recall and reevaluation allows one to put away the pain for a while, until a wave of new memories return that are reexperienced, reevaluated, and redigested. This part of the grieving process occurs in waves. These waves assume different characteristics (particularly, intensity and frequency) over time. The frequency of these experiences gradually decreases, so that by 14 to 16 months the survivors find themselves less haunted by them.

The cancer death bereavement process requires integrating many emotionally powerful experiences into one's ongoing life. It is not, as often popularly believed, an experience of "getting over" something.

One does not "get over" a chronic illness or the eventual death of a loved one. One learns to live with the images, the pain, the sadness, and, not infrequently, the moments of anger.

When death has been the result of a prolonged chronic illness, as for many cancer patients, people wonder how long it takes a person to be emotionally ready to go on with their lives, openly taking in and truly forming new relationships, new connections. When the individual lost is a spouse or best friend, the grieving process continues actively and in very identifiable ways for many years after the death of a loved one. This is a process of integrating (making part of one's memories and emotional self the illness and the death) the entire experience. Never should it be labeled as a "getting over" process.

Over time, for most individuals, the roller coaster of emotions and memories—the chronic illness, its unpleasantness, and the memory of the death itself—has somewhat faded. They are no longer part of the forefront of the lives of survivors, no matter how close they were to the deceased. However, the powerfulness of the feelings, including the grief feelings, remains. A scene from a movie, a passage in a book, a special occasion, a passing image, will suddenly access that reservoir of memories, causing the grief to briefly flow to the surface. Sometimes those memories, and the feelings associated with them, can have an intense, volcanic powerfulness, surging forward on thoughts of supposedly long-past experiences. With patience they subside and seal over again.

These strong memories can be triggered even decades after the events, as powerful and as fresh as they were days or weeks after the loss. When this occurs in the life of a survivor it is often astonishing and sometimes frightening. Survivors should be encouraged to see such experiences as another part of the ongoing process of living with memories, living with our own personal time machines.

Survivors should not be scared by intense memories combined with long-forgotten feelings. Rather, these events can be opportunities to reexamine the feelings, the memories, the experiences with the deceased. One does not need to fight being flooded by them. Survivors may find it helpful to talk about memories with others, or write or reflect or meditate or pray. And, in doing so, they will find that with each resurgence of memory they become more and more able to carry on with, and engage in, life despite their loss and grief. Remembering then becomes a way to honor the lives of those who have died, for survivors are reminded that these memories remain until their own deaths.

Modulated Mourning: The Grief and Mourning of Those Infected and Affected by HIV/AIDS

8

Inge B. Corless, R.N., Ph.D., F.A.A.N.

On Columbus Day weekend 1996, the AIDS Quilt (formally the Names Project Foundation AIDS Memorial Quilt) was exhibited in its entirety on the Mall in Washington, D.C. It had been four years since it was last shown in Washington and it was said that, given its size, it would be the last time. There were panels for 40,000 individuals displayed over an area of almost one mile—the sad evidence of the lethality of this epidemic. Mourners came from far and near to give collective expression and personal presence to the human devastation created by this worldwide pandemic.

The AIDS Quilt, the brainchild of Cleve Jones, himself an HIV (human immunodeficiency virus) infected individual, has translated the mourning of those affected by acquired immunodeficiency syndrome (AIDS) into a public event. The symbolism and beauty of the Quilt with its panels representing adults, children, and infants, and the associated candlelight marches, speeches and discussions that take place when the Quilt is displayed, provide a protected environment for the expression of grief and the display of mourning.

Outside such a gathering, a death related to HIV disease has remained controversial, thereby modulating the expression both of personal grief and of public mourning. The term *grief*, in this chapter, is used to indicate the personal, affective responses to a death. *Mourning*, on the other hand, refers to the public demonstration of being bereaved, of having sustained the death of a loved one. Mourning encompasses the societal expectation of behavior appropriate to such a status and the social support generally available to the bereaved person. The term *modulation* is used to depict the variability of expectation and expression of public behaviors associated with a death from HIV/AIDS.

Although the mourning has become increasingly public and open, as with the display of the Quilt, it remains controversial if not stigmatized. Because of the nature of the disease, as well as other factors such as the lack of socially acknowledged or validated relationships, bereaved individuals may not feel comfortable with publicly expressing their grief, nor may they find a helpful level of support. Thus, their mourning is modulated.

One of the critical aspects of the ritual around the display of the Quilt is that it provides opportunities for the expression of grief in a supportive environment. For many, while the Quilt is acceptable, the cause for the mourning has remained suspect. This issue is the main focus of this chapter and will be addressed shortly.

First, a little background on the Quilt. A Quilt panel is stitched together by significant others, family members, friends, and sometimes strangers, of the person who has died as a result of HIV/AIDS. Typically the work of those who loved the deceased individual, a Quilt panel expresses aspects of the life of the individual being honored. Hobbies, interests, occupations, and family relationships, as well as the date of birth and date of death, are included in these creative and colorful expressions of love and concern. Feathers, sequins, and other decorations festoon some panels; other panels display pictures or momentos meaningful to the individual honored; yet other panels are austere in their simplicity, mentioning only the name and relevant dates.

Sometimes individuals who have already sustained the loss of a loved one as a result of AIDS may work together to create a Quilt panel for an individual who would otherwise go unrecognized. However, the overwhelming majority—namely, 90% of the individuals who have died of HIV/AIDS—are not represented by a Quilt panel.

It is easy to underestimate the devastation that has occurred if one looks only at the numbers represented by the Quilt.

Occasionally, some individuals have more than one panel in their honor. This often happens when the individuals are well-known such as Elizabeth Glaser, the AIDS activist and wife of actor Paul Michael Glaser, and their daughter Ariel. Whether the individual is honored by one or more panels, each panel is carefully indexed as to the donor and the honoree.

Quilt panels are accepted from diverse individuals and groups whose commonality is the creation of a material demonstration of affection and respect. These bonds of grief are further united by the stigmatized cause for the mourning. Unfortunately, a death which results from HIV infection is still perceived with apprehension. In the next section of this paper, community responses, as they affect the grief and mourning of those bereaved through HIV/AIDS, will be explored.

Community Responses to HIV/AIDS

Although groups who have been disproportionately affected by HIV/AIDS will be mentioned, it needs to be stressed that it is only those members of the group who engage in behaviors that put them at risk who have become infected. Such risk factors include: sexual intercourse with an infected partner; the sharing of HIV-contaminated needles; the use of tainted blood or blood products; or being born to an HIV-infected mother or receiving her breast milk. Even in these instances, some people have engaged in these behaviors and not become infected. At a minimum, it is individual behavior, not group identification, that is significant for contracting HIV infection. From an epidemiological perspective, however, certain networks increase the likelihood of HIV infection given that more of their members are already infected. It is important to recognize that the same behaviors may or may not result in infection depending on a number of factors (such as whether the contact is with an HIV-infected person, the size of the inoculum, the amount of the viral load of the infected person, the strain of HIV, the mode of exposure, and the immune status of the recipient). What most HIV-infected individuals share, whether they were the recipients of blood or blood products that were presumed safe or engaged in sexual or needle-sharing behaviors, is that they, likely, were not prepared for such an outcome.

Some reading this chapter might be puzzled by the combining of those who contracted the disease by engaging in socially unsanctioned behaviors such as sexual acts (particularly homosexual acts) or injecting drug use, and those who have contracted it through birth or contaminated blood products. It is this reaction that some are "innocent" victims while others are not that deprives families and significant others of the support customarily provided to those who have experienced the death of a loved one. And knowing of the ostracism of those considered to have engaged in unsanctioned behaviors, the survivors modulate their responses and behaviors so that others will not discover their "secret." Even those deemed "innocent," as well as their survivors, may feel tarnished by the opprobrium given this disease.

It is no wonder that in the recent past (and in some places still today), the families of those who died of AIDS noted the cause of death in the obituary as cancer, pneumonia or lung disease. Moreover, most newspapers did not list the name of the surviving partner in a gay or unmarried relationship, thereby eliminating that person as a legitimate recipient of condolences. Truly, the invisible person. More recently, the term "long-term companion" has been used to describe such relationships. It is a term that is suitable to describe both homosexual and heterosexual relationships.

The cover-up regarding the cause of death may extend to physicians who might list the cause of death of an HIV-infected individual as, in essence, "stopped breathing" or "heart stopped." While this listing may be true, it is less than candid, and certainly not helpful to an accurate accounting of those who have succumbed to this disease. Years ago, similar euphemisms such as "long illness" were used to describe cancer deaths, when those deaths too might cause fear and ostracism. Physicians, family members, and others would have no need for such subterfuge in a more accepting, less judgmental social environment.

The social environment, then, inhibits or facilitates the acknowledgment of bereavement, mourning and grief. What Doka (1989) refers to as *disenfranchised grief* captures the essence of this idea very effectively. The circumstances surrounding a death, and particularly one's formal (and legal) relationship with the deceased, determine whether or not one is permitted to exhibit grief and be recognized as being in a state of mourning. This situation is precisely the one in which many gay men have found themselves. It is also the situation of many women or men in long-term heterosexual relationships.

The question of the acknowledgment and visibility of the individual with a personal relationship that has quasi-public recognition is usually left to the discretion of the "legitimate" heirs. In the situation of the late Audrey Hepburn, on the other hand, it was her consort, Robert Wolders, who sat in the front seat with Ms. Hepburn's sons. Seeing Mel Ferrer, Ms. Hepburn's first husband, sitting in the back of the small church, Mr. Wolders brought him forward and had him sit with the family—an expression of both religious and social grace and solicitude.

Being stigmatized, gay men who have had devoted relationships with their partners may suddenly find that they have little say in the funeral or memorial services and may even be excluded from attending them. If permitted to attend, they may find themselves at the back of the church (symbolically) without recognition of the important role they have played in the life of the deceased. In addition, they may lose not only the sympathy of the community but access to the worldly goods that they had jointly acquired.

This situation is similar to that of the young widow, never fully accepted by her husband's family, who is ostracized by the family immediately upon his death. It indicates the power that the legal system accords blood and legally-sanctioned, socially acceptable relationships. The question of who is the heir and has legitimacy in the public's recognition as a rightful mourner is key to the receipt of the support so helpful to the resolution of grief. In those situations where the bereaved is not accorded the public status of a mourner, he or she is doubly bereaved, contributing to a more complicated grieving process.

This however is the relatively simple situation in which the bereaved mourns one loss. How much more difficult it becomes when multiple losses are experienced. These losses are experienced at a time of potentially diminished physical and financial resources, making accommodation all the more challenging. The loss of both physical vigor and social networks reduces the capacity for grief resolution. Such a situation is similar to that of elderly persons who experience the deaths of loved ones and acquaintances, ultimately shrinking their network of peer relationships.

Those men who have faced the deaths of countless friends and acquaintances find they need to give themselves respite from attending funerals and wakes. They have experienced so many deaths that it is like a river after excessive rains; there is a need to shut off additional flow. When there is so much tragedy, one gets to the point where one can incorporate no more. One hears but does not absorb. The situation is similar to being shell-shocked; one can grieve no more because one is in a state of perpetual grieving.

Sanders' (1989) integrative theory of bereavement, a five-phase theory not unlike that propounded by Elizabeth Kubler-Ross, provides a framework for the further exploration of multiple loss. The five phases are: *shock, awareness of loss, conservation-withdrawal, healing* and *renewal.* Shock is characterized by feelings of confusion, disbelief, restlessness and unreality. Awareness of loss, as the term suggests, is typified by an intense separation anxiety. This leads to the third phase—a need to withdraw. The despair of this phase culminates in a decision to go on or to remain in a state of bereavement. In the fourth phase, healing, the survivor begins to develop a life without the deceased. Finally, in the phase of renewal, the individual has a new sense of the self and purpose in living.

A study by Cherney and Verhey (1996) of multiple loss among gay men found that what they term a process of *habituation* may be occurring, and that the men who participated in their study may be remaining in the third phase of bereavement, namely conservation-withdrawal. What is interesting in the research by Cherney and Verhey is that grief intensity was unrelated to the number of losses. Although there have been comparisons by gay men of the number of losses sustained, individuals reach a threshold of saturation where the capacity to integrate any more loss is reduced. This capacity would differ according to a number of personality traits. For one person, one loss conceivably could create as much upheaval as would occur when another individual had experienced many times that number.

Caring for a dying partner was found to be helpful to the grieving process. But what if both partners are ill? This is not unlike the situation in which many elderly persons find themselves. Guilt about whether the individual did all that was possible may complicate the grieving process. In some situations this guilt is overridden by anger that the partner knowingly, or otherwise, transmitted the infection to the survivor. While in the majority of cases transmission was not intended, unfortunately in some cases it was. Such an action, while rare, nonetheless does damage. The person infected as a result then has his or her own anger with which to deal.

In addition, there is some strain in the gay community between individuals who are HIV-negative and individuals who are HIV-positive. This strain may manifest itself in different political priorities as well as in access to and need for distinct services. As a consequence, gay men may be grieving not only for their lovers, partners, and brethren but also for the loss of community.

In addition to the deaths experienced individually, there is the background of loss experienced by the community. And while an individual may not sustain a loss in a given time period, his friends and acquaintances may be experiencing the deaths of their partners, lovers, friends, and acquaintances. It is the background "noise" of death, combined with what was at one time a lack of treatment options, that also contributed to the air of gloom which pervaded the lives of gay men and others in communities where the disease is epidemic.

Gay men who have encountered difficulty in grieving due to living through so much loss are not unlike soldiers who ultimately experience Posttraumatic Stress Disorder. Soldiers are not encouraged to grieve their losses while they are combatants. Repressing much of their experience, it is only later, away from the battlefield, that the horrors of war and loss manifest themselves. It is likely that gay men who have experienced multiple loss may encounter a similar problem. The major difference is that soldiers are given somewhat greater acceptance than are gays, who are considered to have brought this situation upon themselves. This punishment mentality of "blaming the victim" isolates gay men, depriving them of the social support accorded other bereaved persons. Social support is thus only available from others in the gay network who may themselves be depleted from the numerous losses experienced.

From another perspective, the family that ostracizes the partner of their son loses a valuable resource for a continuing bond with their son and the man with whom their son has developed a valued relationship. By cutting themselves off from this aspect of their son's development, families lose connection with their son's present life and are restricted to a past of their own making. As ostensibly comforting as this may appear, it reduces the potential sources of support. Unfortunately, families often elect such a restricted perspective in order to assure support from their own social network.

Those who are courageous enough to publicly acknowledge their son have been surprised by the support they have received. For example, a family whose son had died published a notice in the post office about his death from AIDS and the date and time of the upcoming memorial. They did not know whether the townspeople would come. The people of the town came; the church was filled to overflowing. The Lutheran and Methodist church women even joined together to prepare the refreshments. "There was sadness there, but you could see and feel the healing that was taking place. Months of silence and suffering could finally be shared" (Mims, 1994).

Communities differ. Not all families would encounter a similar degree of acceptance and support. Perhaps it was because these parents acknowledged their son that others were free to do so as well. Clearly, the leadership of influential members of the community makes a difference. It has often been said, for example, that had President Reagan invited the Ray family to stay with him until local housing was secured, he would have set an example for all to follow. The Ray family had three hemophiliac sons who became HIV-infected from contaminated blood products. When this situation became public knowledge, their house was set on fire. The response of local community public health and political leaders was inadequate. It is here where an individual of President Reagan's stature could have made a crucial difference for all of those infected and affected by HIV disease, and indeed for the nation.

The Ray children, like at least 10,000 hemophiliacs, were infected through their use of contaminated Factor VIII preparations. Factor VIII inhibits the bleeding which hemophiliacs experience due to a lack of clotting factor in their blood. The advent of Factor VIII provided an almost normal life style to individuals who were otherwise restricted in their activities lest they incur a bleeding episode, which could be life-threatening.

The very resources to whom hemophiliacs had turned for assistance—the government, science, and medicine—were perceived not to have protected them from assault from this new and unsuspected source. Physicians, who at last had something to offer their hemophiliac patients, were reluctant to return to pre-Factor medical care and, in some cases, were not as vigilant as would have been prudent.

Those Hemophilia Center physicians who had dedicated themselves and their careers to the care of hemophiliacs confronted a special grief as they watched the patients for whom they had cared over the years perish as a result of contaminated blood products. And the families of the hemophiliacs felt betrayed by a system that was supposed to care for them. Anger mixed with grief and the question of whether something more could have been done complicates the resolution of grief. And while the death of a hemophiliac carries no public onus, infection with HIV does. Even though hemophiliacs' families have been accorded more respect in their mourning, there is nonetheless part of the stigma associated with having succumbed to HIV disease.

The situation of minorities in lower-income communities is yet more complex. Faced with poverty, violence, a lack of opportunity and ill health, these individuals confront many complex situations with few resources. At the same time, they are bombarded with images of life styles and worldly goods on television, in the movies and in stores, which may not be part of their immediate lives. Some perceive their avenue to advancement in terms of alternative economic practices, mainly in the distribution of street drugs, car thefts and other forms of illegitimate activities. It is this context in which injecting drug use and the subsequently high rates of HIV infection often occur.

Feeling that they will not live until they are twenty-five changes the calculus of risktaking. It is not a question of not recognizing the danger—these youngsters are overwhelmed by danger. Whereas young people in more affluent neighborhoods may feel they will live forever and so that nothing they do is a risk, the situation in lower-income communities is such that nothing that young people, especially young men, can do changes the fact that at any time they may be killed. They know all too well they won't live forever; longer-term planning under such circumstances seems absurd.

Families are grieving the losses of their young people through violence, through incarceration for crimes alleged or committed, through drug-related deaths, and through HIV/AIDS. This is the experience of loss from multiple causes. Some families have grandmothers caring for the children in the family because the parents are absent, in jail, on drugs, or sick with HIV/AIDS or some other disease. In some cases, both parents and children are HIV-infected. Thus, death and loss touch both the family and the community.

In the gay community, bereavement tends to occur among members of the same generation. In communities where injecting drug use is high, members of different generations of a family are dying of the same disease. Infected mothers may be caring for their infected children, hoping to live long enough to be present throughout the course of their children's disease. Often, the mothers precede their offspring in death and arrangements need to be made for the children. When a family member is not available, a friend may take the children or they may be placed in foster care.

It is estimated that by the year 2000 there will be 75,000 to 125,000 AIDS orphans in the United States, with 60,000 in New York City alone. Some of these youngsters will be HIV-infected, others will not. The uninfected child may be the only one of the family to survive. The tremendous pressure placed on such a child is not unlike that of the survivor of a tragic accident that kills an entire family except for one or two persons. The potential for a heavy burden of survivorship guilt is very real. And the grief of having one's parents die of a stigmatized disease, and then to experience the death of a brother or sister as well, increases the burden.

Responses to the Terminally Ill and Bereaved

What then can be done to facilitate grief and mourning? Leadership is needed from religious organizations. The more helpful the church or faith community, the easier it will be to acknowledge the nature of the illness besetting the family. Such support not only validates and encourages mourning, it can help individuals wrestle with the deep spiritual issues that may be raised by the death. There are religious communities where such assistance can be secured; in others, support may not be forthcoming. There are also a number of ethnic or social groups that have developed AIDS service organizations. These non-governmental, community-based organizations can help with information and offer a variety of resources.

Leadership at a national level can have a salubrious effect on access to information as well as on the openness with which people display their grief and participate in mourning rituals. As is obvious from the previously-cited example of the church women, such leadership can also be initiated at the local level.

If one assumes that we are indeed our brothers' and sisters' keepers and thus have responsibility each for the other, then we need to reach out with caring to assist those whose burdens are heavy. The partners and families of individuals dying from AIDS need some of the same assistance as does anyone caring for someone with a terminal illness. Some suggestions to consider:

1. Visiting with the sick person so that the caregiver can have some time away;
2. Assisting with errands to relieve the caregiver;
3. Providing transportation to medical appointments;
4. Bringing some favorite foods that can be frozen if not used immediately;
5. Arranging an outing for the person who is ill;
6. Caring for the other children in a family where a child is dying;
7. Arranging for the caregiver to receive needed medical attention.

This short list can easily be supplemented by asking the persons concerned what might be helpful. While some people may be reluctant initially to take advantage of such an offer, assistance may be more readily accepted when it is clear that the offer is genuine. The importance of providing support during the terminal stages of an illness is that there will not be the "If only I had . . . "; that is, there will be no regrets.

Doing is not the only mode of assistance. Being present is a great help. It is bearing witness to one of the great dramas in life, and in fact can be a rehearsal for one's own dying. Most of all, by caring in the present, one avoids the regrets of the future. Such caring will inspire others who are reluctant to overcome their prejudices and fears to reach out to friends, neighbors, family members and hopefully to strangers.

Some of the activities that are helpful during the terminal illness are also useful during bereavement. The grieving individual may be able to find comfort in talking about his or her loss, but it must be at the time the bereaved selects and not when the helper decides it is convenient or necessary. An example of the latter is the student nurse who, on the last day on a given service, went to a patient and said, "Now we have to talk about death and dying." Obviously that approach is neither appropriate nor helpful.

The situation of the dying family where two generations are infected is complex. Issues of the custody of minor children, let alone the status of their health, make for a more difficult problem. Given the numbers of AIDS orphans, there has been talk of resurrecting orphanages. Whatever the ultimate placement of these youngsters, they are grieving the loss of parental figures and are in situations where they are like displaced persons. They not only have lost parental figures but also their place in a family. The support required by such youngsters is substantial. A "Big Sister" or Big Brother" could be of enormous help to such children.

And help is what many persons dying of AIDS require. While there are numerous agencies with programs for the HIV-infected, the resources for those who are bereaved are not as plentiful. Greater attention needs to be given to these individuals.

Conclusion

The display of the Quilt began locally and became a national phenomenon. It has sanctioned the public expression of mourning and the display of AIDS-related grief. A workshop leader of the conference held in conjunction with the exhibiting of the Quilt commented that he thought that there were far more panels evident from the 1980's and fewer from the 1990's. He wondered if the commitment to the making of such panels had diminished with time. He also observed that the once hushed silence of reverence, awe and grief had been replaced with more casual conversation and the bonhomie of an afternoon out. One can only wonder whether the change is the result of the routinization of HIV/AIDS so that it has become part of the background of our lives, or if it is the difference in the socioeconomic background of those more recently dying as a result of AIDS.

It may mean that a Quilt panel will no longer represent the common thread which binds those infected and affected by HIV/AIDS no matter their gender, sexual orientation, age, ethnic, or economic background. The decline in the participation in a common ritual may very well symbolize the continuing isolation of those grieving the death of someone from HIV/AIDS. As the impetus to make a Quilt panel diminishes, this source of comfort to the bereaved is removed.

Perhaps we need to recognize the vital importance that rituals, and in particular the Quilt, can serve—to reaffirm the connectedness of a group composed of some variation of partner, family members, lovers and friends, a connectedness which increases as they work together to create a panel. This final gesture of love enhances the emotional bond of those working on the Quilt panel; it is a most appropriate mourning ritual and should be encouraged. This ritual is one in which we can all participate, perhaps thereby eliminating the need to modulate mourning. Quilting is, after all, an American tradition.

Systemic Understandings of Loss and Grief Related to Alzheimer's Disease

9

Carol Williams, M.S. and
Brenda Moretta, Ph.D.

Alzheimer's disease (AD) is a progressive, fatal illness that afflicts more than four million Americans, ravaging its victims' minds for up to ten or more years. Although the rate of deterioration varies from one person to another, AD follows a progressive path of destruction in all of its victims. What begins as memory problems eventually progresses to a more severe loss of intellectual function as evidenced by mental confusion, problem-solving difficulties, poor judgment, and speech/language deficits. Additionally, AD victims typically experience bladder and bowel incontinence, sleep disturbance, suspiciousness or paranoia, and other significant personality changes. In the latter stages of the disease, the victim is completely disoriented, noncommunicative, and nonambulatory. AD victims experience a loss of intellect, social functioning, self-care ability, behavioral and emotional control, and ultimately, their sense of self (Cohen and Eisdorfer, 1986).

These losses affect both the AD victim and the family throughout the course of the illness. As the disease progresses, the AD victim needs more structure, supervision, and care, which demands increasingly greater financial, emotional, physical, and social investment by the family caregiver(s). In fact, "because of the long term burdens on them and the potential physical and emotional consequences, family members are recognized as the secondary victims of AD" (Darris, 1988, p. 6).

It is important to expand our knowledge of the AD family caregiver experience to include consideration of their loss and grief, because as Collins, Liken, King, and Kokinakis (1993) suggest, "family caregiving and bereavement, often treated as separate events, are, in fact, part of a single, chronic situation" (p. 238).

The following text will address the interrelated processes of AD family caregiving and pre-death bereavement. In doing so, the beginning discussion will identify the multiple losses that AD family caregivers face and will consider how these losses influence the AD family caregivers' anticipatory grief experience. The remaining discourse will examine special issues related to the caregiving process, followed by methods of psychosocial support and family intervention strategies that can be utilized by various disciplines and professionals involved in work with AD victims and their caregivers.

Multiple Losses Related to the AD Family Caregiving Situation

Loss of Relationship

Alzheimer's disease has been recognized as causing the psychological death of its victims long before the actual physical death (Cohen and Eisdorfer, 1986). In fact, Austrom and Hendrie (1990) note that "some caregivers describe the physical death as the second death" (p. 20). As the course of the disease progresses, AD victims lose the ability to recognize and communicate with loved ones; consequently, intimacy, affection, and all meaningful social interaction is lost. In their study of loss and grief in AD family caregivers, Collins et al. (1993) found that 54% of their sample reported a loss of familiarity that harmed their relationship with their loved one. An additional 35% of the sample reported that a breakdown of communication was responsible for the deterioration of the relationship with their AD-afflicted family member. This has a devastating effect on AD family caregivers.

In addition to the communication and recognition breakdown that can destroy relationships, AD victims may also experience significant personality changes which result in uncharacteristic behavioral and mood disturbances. These personality changes are often confusing and painful for family members and may contribute to further relationship breakdown. Persons with AD look the same, but they no longer possess the essence of who they have been throughout their life. It is as if the person the family has known and loved has died and has been replaced by a stranger. A mild-mannered father who was always loving and gentle may now be irritable, hostile, and agitated, swearing at his family and treating them with disrespect and anger. A loving wife may demand that her husband is a stranger who is trying to harm her and she may order him out of their house or call the police to intervene.

However, it may not only be the AD victim who exhibits behavioral and emotional changes. AD may force caregivers to relate or behave in an unfamiliar manner toward the person with AD. A child or spouse may have to relinquish their respective role in order to fulfill a necessary parental role, or they may find themselves behaving in ways that are uncharacteristic and, consequently, disturbing to them.

In sharing his story about the effects of AD on the caregiver, one loving husband talked about his pain and horror over hitting his beloved wife, toward whom he had never raised a hand throughout their forty-two-year marriage. Throughout their marriage, his wife had regularly colored her hair. In an effort to preserve the familiar, the husband continued to color his wife's hair when she become too debilitated to do so herself. Although normally an uneventful process, during one attempt to color her hair she suddenly became frightened and combative and would not allow him to rinse out the color. The husband tried every technique he could think of to calm his wife down, but his attempts were unsuccessful. Soon the color began to burn the wife's scalp and she became even more agitated as she screamed in pain. However, she still would not allow him to remove the color. With no one to assist him, and fearful for her well-being, the man hopelessly hit his wife in an effort to shock her into submission so that he could rinse the color from her hair to stop the burning. The man was not lashing out angrily, nor was he abusive by nature. He was, however, desperate and alone, and he knew of no other way to help his wife. By the end of this tragic ordeal, both husband and wife were sobbing and heartbroken. The husband had not only lost his wife and marriage to AD, but he felt that he had also lost himself along the way. This uncharacteristic behavior contributed to his overwhelming sense of guilt and repulsion.

Family members grieve the loss of the person who used to be and who no longer exists as they once knew them, and they may also grieve the loss of a piece of themselves and the role that they once played in their loved one's life. Consequently, not only does the AD victim lose his or her sense of self, but so too does the caregiver, who may question "Who am I?" or "Who am I in the context of my changing family?" The answers to these questions evolve throughout the course of the disease and the caregiving; sometimes the caregivers' answers are sobering, while at other times the answers seem foreign and unacceptable.

Loss of Social Interaction and Support from Friends and Family

Unfortunately, as caregivers are losing their relationship with their loved one to AD, they may also be losing friends and family due to the consuming nature of the AD caregiving role. The caregiver's lack of availability and energy resulting from caregiving demands may lead them to alienate themselves from others. Friends and family may not understand why the caregiver cannot spare the time to go to a movie or to get together for a meal, or why the caregiver can't leave home to visit with them.

Lack of time and energy may restrict a caregiver's social world, contributing to the decline of social interaction in general. Because caregivers must provide so much routine care and watchful supervision for the AD victim at home, they may restrict their socialization to the parameters of their home. For various reasons, some friends and family may avoid visiting the caregiver at home, which isolates the caregiver from the outside world even more. Sometimes friends do not visit because even though they may understand the effects of

AD, they feel uncomfortable with the AD victim's unusual or inappropriate behaviors.

In a family support group, one member shared that her mother, whom she had cared for over six years, would frequently expose herself and masturbate on the living room sofa. Initially, the mother's behavior embarrassed and shamed her daughter and the daughter's two teenage sons, who would frequently bring friends home after school. However, through education and creative problem-solving strategies provided to family and friends, the family found an acceptable solution that allowed for the sons to continue bringing home friends in spite of their grandmother's behavior. However, were it not for their determination, creativity, and the understanding of friends and family, this woman and her sons would have likely suffered from social isolation over time, as many families do.

It is a bewildering challenge for all involved to adjust to the caregiving demands that result from the gradual physical and psychological death of the person afflicted with AD, because unlike many other chronic, terminal illnesses which leave their victims looking physically ill, AD victims typically look healthy, strong, and "normal." The external appearance of health is incongruent with the devastating destruction actually taking place in the brain of the person suffering from AD (Aronson, 1988). Because the AD victim usually exhibits no external signs of disease and generally appears to be healthy, the family's grief is sometimes misunderstood and/or invalidated by others who do not understand the true nature of the disease. The AD family caregiver, then, becomes a silent mourner who often lives with disenfranchised grief (Doka, 1989).

Doka states that "disenfranchised grief is grief that cannot be openly acknowledged, socially shared, or publicly supported" (1993, p. 193). When an AD victim looks healthy to friends and non-care-providing family members, their "slow death" is ambiguous. Friends and family may not fully comprehend the caregiver's unique loss and grief experiences (Walker, Pomeroy, McNeil, and Franklin, 1994). Consequently, those persons may not assist the caregiver because they do not know that their help is needed.

Furthermore, it is usually difficult for AD caregivers to ask for and receive support from others. Caregivers may be reluctant to openly acknowledge their pain and grief or ask for help because they feel that they should be able to provide all the required assistance. After all, they may have been told that it is "only a cognitive problem." This position may contribute to the caregiver not viewing their loss, grief, and the need for support as legitimate. Walker et al. (1994) and Aronson (1988), on the other hand, suggest that caregivers may not ask for support because AD is a stigmatized illness. Some of the early symptoms of AD mimic mental illness, and AD is associated with the elderly, a group of people in our county who are often stigmatized by the effects of ageism. As a result of the caregiver's shame, guilt, anger or embarrassment, AD caregivers may not seek out support or acknowledge their grief.

No matter what the reason for the loss of social interaction and support, it is unfortunate that as the disease progresses and as the demands of caregiving increase, opportunities for socialization with family and friends grow scarcer at the very time the caregiver needs more support. The loss of the relationship with the AD victim is heartbreaking, and the additional loss of supportive relationships can isolate and overwhelm the caregiver and contribute to the role of the silent mourner.

Loss of the Opportunity for Closure and Completion of Unfinished Business

Due to the insidious nature of AD, it is easy for families to deny the seriousness of the illness in addition to the long-term implications of the disease (Aronson, 1988; Austrom and Hendrie, 1990). Some caregivers wait too long to share unspoken feelings, make important arrangements, discuss unresolved issues, and say their good-byes to the AD victim. If feelings, thoughts, and words are left unspoken, caregivers may experience grief, remorse, and guilt when they suddenly realize it is too late to tell the AD victim all they wanted to say. A family support group member, upon recognition that her mother could no longer comprehend conversations, stated, "I never really knew how bad Mom was, and by the time I did, it was too late to tell her how much she meant to me and what a really good mother she had always been to us kids. Her last memories were probably of me yelling at her to stop asking me what time it was."

During the years of caring for a loved one with AD, many situations arise which may result in feelings of anger, frustration, fear, loneliness, guilt, and shame. Under normal conditions, when one's interactions with others result in strong emotions and conflict, there is an opportunity to process those feelings. However, as the preceding example illustrates, with AD there comes a time when there is no longer an opportunity for discussion and closure related to many day-to-day issues. The loss of opportunity to say goodbye, to make important arrangements, and to process one's emotions with the AD victim may complicate caregivers' grief if they do not have appropriate means by which to release and share their feelings and thoughts.

Loss of One's Own Health

AD caregivers often reach a point where they experience a health crisis due to the overwhelming physical and emotional demands of the caregiver role. In Collins et al.'s (1993) study of AD family caregivers, 32% of their sample reported that their grief was compounded by the physical and emotional fatigue related to their caregiving role. These same authors quote one of their participants as saying, "I was stretched physically, emotionally, and spiritually. Caregiving drained me, and I was exhausted" (p. 244). Such a sentiment is echoed by many caregivers. In the authors' experience, one common predictor of nursing home placement is the primary caregiver's physical disability as the patient care demands increase. Collins et al.'s research supports this view. In fact, some caregivers who participated in their study expressed relief that their loved one had died before they were so physically and emotionally depleted that they had to consider placing them in a nursing home.

Many caregivers are elderly themselves, and the demands of providing around-the-clock care can exhaust their already limited physical resources. Also, many AD victims sleep very little during the night and are irritable and restless throughout the evening hours. As a result, the caregiver typically does not get an adequate amount of sleep because they must remain vigilant during what becomes a "36-hour day" (Mace and Rabins, 1981). Such intensive caregiving takes its toll, both physically and psychologically, over time. Many caregivers reach a point where they simply cannot provide home-based care any longer and they must consider nursing home placement. Such a decision, however, is not reached easily.

Loss Related to Institutionalization

Most people never intend to place their loved one in a nursing home. This decision is rarely made without feelings of intense guilt and fear. "If I were a good daughter," one caregiver said, "I would be able to take care of Mother at home. She always took care of me. When things got tough for her when I was a child, she just didn't send me away. She made many sacrifices for me. The least I can do is give that same love back to her." Many family members and friends believe that making the decision to place their loved one in an institution means that they must not be demonstrating their love to the AD victim. This, in turn, contributes to a tremendous amount of guilt and shame on behalf of the caretaker. Many times, the caregiver is criticized by other family members and friends of the AD victim who do not understand the severity of the disease, causing intrafamilial distances as well as friendship detachments. The caregiver feels even more isolated, inadequate, guilty, and remorseful. Contact is sometimes severed between the primary caregiver and other family members and friends, further contributing to the disenfranchised grief that develops.

It is at this point that the institution's staff begins to see the discontent between the various family members and friends, and their interventions, although well-meaning, often serve to create a bigger gap between those who love the AD victim. The staff may then begin to attach themselves emotionally to the AD victim in an effort to provide the individual with a sense of love and family unity, thus creating a context for the staff members themselves to experience the effects of disenfranchised grief. Staff members are told to mind their own business when they have strong opinions about the care of the AD victim, and especially when they share their opinions with family members or friends. Although this is not always the case, and the messages that are sent to the staff members about keeping their opinions to themselves are subtle, they are indeed present.

One daughter of an AD victim recalled this event during a converstation with one of the authors: "The aide was telling me that my mother no longer liked to eat ice cream. Mother always ate ice cream after supper each night. I know my mother. This aide has only known my mother for one year. So when I tell her to feed my mother ice cream, she needs to do it!" As the aide overheard this conversation, she silently got up from feeding the AD victim, discreetly walked to an empty room and began to weep. The daughter sat down next to her mother and attempted to feed her the ice cream. As the daughter smiled and talked to her in a calm relaxing voice, the AD victim gazed at her once familiar daughter with a blank stare. "But Mother," the daughter said, "you've always loved ice cream and this is your favorite flavor. Please open your mouth, Mother. I want you to be happy. I love you." The AD victim responded by saying, "It's a very nice day." Tears began to stream down the daughter's face as she quietly excused herself from the dining area and left the facility.

The aide and the daughter were both experiencing the effects of disenfranchised grief. Onlookers could not understand why the daughter was "so emotional." They even volunteered to eat the ice cream, since the AD victim obviously would not. The daughter could not understand why the aide was so "rude and insensitive." Neither the aide nor the daughter were given permission to be sad about the subtle losses they were experiencing. The aide was deprived of feeling connected to the AD victim because she had only known the AD victim for a relatively short time. The daughter's sadness was not validated because the incident was "trivial," according to the nursing staff who had more important issues to attend to.

Intervening with Caregivers

The disenfranchised nature of the AD family caregiver's grief, combined with the progressive, lengthy nature of AD, and a plethora of AD victim and caregiver losses, all contribute to what family members often express as witnessing their loved one's "living funeral" (Cohen and Eisdorfer, 1986, p. 267). This sentiment was reinforced by an AD family support group member when she stated that "a part of me dies every day as I watch my husband, my lifelong companion, lover, and confidant slip away a little piece at a time." This "living funeral" provides a backdrop for a unique anticipatory grief process, one that could benefit from psychosocial intervention for the patient and family.

Scenarios similar to the incident above contribute to increased feelings of guilt over the decision to place a family member in an institution. They also serve as indications, subtle to some of the paid caregiving staff and obvious to many family members, of the progressive losses that occur over and over again as the AD victim deteriorates ever so gradually. Consequently, the caregiver grieves repeatedly and the goodbye is prolonged as they lose their loved one slowly and laboriously. Many family members have talked about this process in terms of "saying a long goodbye." The process of grief endures from the time an individual is diagnosed with AD until well after the AD victim has died.

The paid caregiving staff can help ease the pain of these long goodbyes through various interventions. Educating the caregivers is the first step toward this end. Doug Manning (1983) describes love as doing what people need, not just what the AD victim wants, and not just what the caregivers want. It is important to tell caregivers that institutions can provide services that the family cannot. They have around-the-clock nurses on duty, specially designed bath facilities, and a wide variety of stimulating activities for social interaction and the preservation of fine and gross motor skills, cognitive skills, ambulatory ability, and spirituality.

In their reluctance to place their loved one in a nursing facility, caregivers often present themselves to others as willing to take care of the AD victim no matter what the cost. This cost is never the caregiver's alone. It takes the caregiver away from their privacy, their own social contact, and their own family obligations. The caregiver's career often becomes a lower priority, which may result in negative economic and employment consequences. The physical consequences can also take their toll on the caregiver, as already mentioned. The primary caregiver is usually exhausted at the end of each day, but must then muster up the energy to meet his or her own family's needs.

Professionals working with the families of AD victims should anticipate asking the families general and practical questions in an effort to demonstrate their understanding and empathy for the caregiver's situation, while recognizing the possible ramifications of the caregiver's decisions. Whether the caregiver chooses to place the AD victim in a nursing facility or continue to care for the individual in their own home, it is advisable for the professional to adopt a humanistic stance rather than a marketing and recruitment stance.

Various cultures have different expectations for the care of their elderly. Professionals can ask about these cultural expectations in a respectful and open manner. Questions can be posed such as: What does your family think about the possibility of placing your loved one in a nursing facility? What will others think about you if you decide to admit your loved one to a facility? What kinds of things has your family done in the past in similar situations? What do you think is expected of your family from others within your neighborhood, church, or social group? How do you think they might take this?

This line of questioning gives the caregiver the message that it is understood that their decision will affect many people, and that the professional working with them is sensitive to this issue. It can also contribute to creating and establishing a trusting relationship between the professional and caregiver.

Asking the caregiver to imagine themselves as the AD victim and to think about what they would want in this situation can also be helpful at times. On the other hand, it can also solidify the caregiver's guilt and add to their increasing sense of debt toward their loved one. Nevertheless, this information can be useful. It can give the caregiver a renewed sense of peace and energy, knowing that they are doing the best they can to care for their loved one, given their limitations.

Family conferences should be held on a regular basis to discuss the AD victim's status. This is an opportunity to invite relatives and friends who want to participate in the decisionmaking process to feel connected and to develop a sense that they are important to the family and to the AD victim. This group should not always focus on decisionmaking, problem solving, and sharing concerns related to the AD victim. These important issues can certainly be components of the group, but the group should also use this time to share special stories about the AD victim—from the past and the present. The conferences can be led by a professional or by family and friends taking turns as group leaders. Some might call this a therapy group, and in essence it is. However, some families may respond better if it is called a "meeting" or "conference" rather than "therapy."

Family Considerations

It is not uncommon for family members and friends to work together to hide the symptoms of their loved one's AD from others. The diagnosis of AD sits on a fence, conceptually, for many people. It is a medical condition, but it is also listed in the American Psychiatric Association's Diagnostic and Statistical Manual of Mental Disorders IV (1995). Psychiatrists, physicians, psychologists, therapists and social workers all have the expertise to diagnose AD under their specialized licenses. It is important to remember that caregivers are often surprised and ashamed at the behavior of the AD victim. Sometimes bizarre behaviors associated with the AD victim's personality disintegration may resemble paranoia and features of schizophrenia as well as behaviors that appear to be delusions and hallucinations.

This can be very frightening for family and friends. Many may seriously question the possibility of the AD victim being mentally ill. Family and friends slowly begin to become organized around the problem: AD and the victim's way of manifesting his or her illness. Consequently, the family dynamics change and the entire family system changes. People engage in conversations with themselves and others about what is happening and they begin to develop particular meanings about what the "problem" really is (Anderson and Goolishian, 1991; Biever, Gardner, and Bobele, 1995; Gergen, 1985; Hoffman, 1990). From the beginning, the situation is defined as a "problem" rather than an "illness" (Parry and Doan, 1994; Rosenblatt, 1994; Shotter, 1992).

Sometimes the family may organize around denial and may all participate in creating a context in which the denial can exist (Wyne,

Weber and McDaniel, 1986). This has the potential of exacerbating the denial by interfering with the safety of the AD victim. However, denial may also help the family cope with the pain. It reduces the grieving in the family, especially since families of AD victims have to endure an extended grieving process. Family resources can paradoxically be discovered as a result of denial. The family may look for ways to accommodate the AD victim's behavior, focusing primarily on the positive aspects of that behavior. In these cases, denial is not necessarily a defense that the professional should feel obligated to help the family break through; it may be serving a very important function for that family.

Therapy can be a way for family and friends to sort through their confused emotions and understandings (Keizer and Feins, 1991). The therapist can facilitate a conversation to create new meaning for the client. Some helpful questions are: What do you think is preventing your family from accepting the diagnosis? How will you know when your family will be ready to accept the changes, if ever? What has to happen for your family to be able to accept the diagnosis as well as the changes you see in the AD victim?

These questions lead to a safer conversation for those in denial, particularly unhelpful denial, because it centers around preparation, rather than pushing for acceptance. When the family understands their state as one of "preparation," it takes the pressure away from them to have to accept what may never be acceptable. It frees the family up to be able to enjoy the moment-to-moment interactions with their loved one.

The role of the therapist is to help the family create new meanings and understandings about the AD victim's circumstances, which gently aid the family in accepting the AD victim for where they are in their disease process on any given day (Anderson, 1986; Anderson and Goolishian, 1988). One way to accomplish this is to facilitate the family's telling and re-telling of their story (Parry and Doan, 1994). Questions can be asked about how each family member is affected by the other family members' ways of understanding the situation. The following open-ended questions presume a positive outcome from a devastating illness for which it is difficult to see much hope: What is it like for you to have to come to visit Dad in a nursing home? How have your family priorities shifted? How has this helped your family become more cohesive? What strengths and resources have you discovered in your family that you didn't know you had? It seems like a lot of control has been lost, but what do you have control over? What are some things, other than recovery, that you can control?

Many authors suggest that loss characterizes the totality of the experience for Alzheimer's family caregivers. While loss is an important component, it is not the totality of the experience. It is essential to address the loss, but it is equally important to identify family resources, so they can be expanded upon during this long and difficult period. Family loss can be addressed in many ways. One way to look at loss is in a family group setting. Each family member is asked to bring an item to the next meeting that reminds them of who the AD victim was, is, and how they would like to remember them, without telling other family members what the item is. At the following meeting, each family member shares the item and their rationale for choosing that particular item, as well as their thoughts and feelings about the item. This item has the potential for becoming a very important symbol, or linking object, for the family member, particularly after the AD victim dies.

Grief can enhance the growth of the family system. It is the therapist's task to work with the family to find ways for them to stay connected to the living parts of the AD victim, well after the living death, and eventually the physical death, has occurred. Even though the personality of the person who once occupied the body of the AD victim seems to be distant and perhaps even lost long before the physical death occurs, the essence of the caregiver's loved one can be preserved and honored with every thought and memory of them. Grieving makes happiness possible, particularly the happiness associated with the caregiver's recognition that they had the privilege of knowing and loving the AD victim. These lessons of love can then be transmitted generationally as the family system grows in number and in cohesiveness.

PART III

Paths to Healing

A final section considers ways to help the bereaved. Corr's chapter begins this section with a sage reminder not to neglect the needs of children and adolescents as they cope with the long-term illness and death of a person in their world. He reminds us that children's responses, too, are unique—influenced by the relationship to the dying person, the mode of death, the child's coping strategies, the age and development of the child, and the availability of support.

Grollman offers a path to healing in his chapter by emphasizing the importance of finding ways to nourish oneself spiritually, and sustain oneself emotionally, in loss.

Neimeyer offers another path to healing. He defines grieving as a way of reconstructing meaning after a loss. His approach acknowledges the power of spiritual and cognitive processes as one grieves.

A third path is suggested by Zulli and Weeks. Their chapter on ritual demonstrates the critical role that rituals can have in resolving loss. This approach, while drawing on the spiritual, is primarily a behavioral response.

All three chapters reinforce the idea that prolonged illness provides opportunity for therapeutic intervention both during and after the illness. These three approaches are examples of a range of interventive strategies, some of which are discussed in prior sections. These approaches are complementary; for example, masculine grievers (Martin and Doka, 1995) may find cognitive and behavioral approaches more compatible with their coping styles. The critical question remains: "What paths to wholeness and healing will this particular survivor find most helpful?"

Coping with Long-term Illness and Death in an Adult: The Impact on Grieving Children and Adolescents

10

Charles A. Corr

Coping with long-term illness and the extended processes of dying that are associated with chronic or degenerative diseases is a common feature of encounters with death in industrialized countries near the close of the 20th century. When this experience involves a parent, grandparent, or other significant adult, it clearly has an impact on the grief of children and adolescents. This chapter describes that impact and shows how helpers can assist grieving children or adolescents who are coping with long-term illness and death in an adult.

Five main factors stand out in all experiences of grief (Corr, Nabe, and Corr, 1997). They are:

1. the nature of the prior attachment to the ill, dying, or deceased person;
2. the mode of death and concurrent circumstances of the survivor;
3. the coping strategies that the child or adolescent has learned to use in managing previous losses;
4. the developmental situation of the particular child or adolescent; and

5. the availability and nature of support during the illness or following the death.

These five factors serve here to organize the analysis that follows.

Prior Attachments

Understanding Prior Attachments

Attachments are the special relationships that serve to satisfy basic human needs. Among many other interpersonal bonds, a young child may have a casual relationship with someone in his or her immediate neighborhood, just as an older child may have a functional relationship with an administrator in his or her school. But attachments to a parent or a classroom teacher are likely to be more fundamental and meaningful in the child or adolescent's life.

Attachments are significant for all human beings, but especially for children and adolescents. Adults are often able to form alternative attachments or find other ways to satisfy their needs when a particular attachment ends or is no longer satisfactory. Children and adolescents, however, are likely to be far more dependent on a limited set of attachments and may lack the ability to seek out substitute attachments on their own.

Several features of attachments are of special importance for understanding grieving children and adolescents. Where there has been no significant attachment or prior relationship, there is likely to be no prominent grief reaction. Children and adolescents do not grieve losses that are not meaningful to them. Some attachments are only fully appreciated after they have ended. When the attachment figure has been a constant and reliable presence in the life of a child or adolescent, it may not have been fully evident prior to a death how important that presence truly was.

Attachments are commonly depicted as warm, nurturing relationships. In fact, however, this is not always the case. A child or adolescent may be dependent upon an indifferent mother who is distracted by depression or the use of addictive drugs, or upon an abusive father who takes out his own frustrations on younger members of his family. Not surprisingly, disruptions in or the termination of such an attachment may leave the bereaved child or adolescent with a complicated and difficult grief reaction.

Attachments often involve many dimensions or levels of interaction between a child or adolescent and the attachment figure. In such circumstances, the grief reaction to the loss of such an attachment can also be expected to be multidimensional and complex. A bereaved child or adolescent is likely to grieve or respond (perhaps over time) to each aspect of what has been lost in the ending of the attachment. Insofar as that child or adolescent is able to do so, he or she will mourn or strive to cope with each important aspect of the lost attachment and its related grief reaction.

Helping with Prior Attachments

Helpers should explore with the bereaved child or adolescent his or her attachment to the ill or deceased person. In order to initiate any helpful intervention, it is critical to gain some appreciation of the child or adolescent's perception of the attachment, both in itself and in its role as a foundation for grief. This can be done by listening carefully to the child or adolescent's expressions of grief and to his or her comments about the attachment figure. Gentle inquiries may take the form of a series of questions, such as the following: What did you most like or dislike about the attachment figure? What is it that you miss now? Why do you miss those aspects of the severed attachment? Are there other aspects that you do not miss?

Over time, a helper might begin to ask additional questions, such as: How has your life been changed by the illness or death of the loved person? How has your family been changed? Who takes care of your needs now? What alternative attachments have been established in your life to meet your needs? What other attachments might be established? Verbal questions of this sort are, of course, only one way of eliciting an appreciation of the ways in which prior attachments have been altered by illness and death. Some helpers who work with grieving children and adolescents have used art, play, puppets and other modes of symbolic interaction to serve these purposes. One of the best known of these techniques is the kinetic family drawing in which the child or adolescent is asked to draw a picture of his or her family before and after the illness/death. The important element in this process is not so much the specific technique used by the adult helper but its effectiveness in assisting the grieving child or adolescent and the helper to appreciate or realize all that was significant in the attachment and all that is equally important in the grief reaction.

In cases of long-term illness and dying, helpful interventions are not confined solely to the post-death period. Often during the dying process, there is a quite understandable tendency to focus on the needs of the dying person. That focus can become problematic when it leads individuals involved to overlook both the everyday needs of children and adolescents and the special issues that they face in connection with the dying of a significant person.

Helpers who come into contact with a bereaved child or adolescent after the death should also inquire about what things were like for the youngster during the dying process and what important changes took place in his or her life before the death. Similarly, when a helper can intervene prior to a death it can be useful to address the needs of the young survivor-to-be, to strive to acknowledge or strengthen healthy bonds with the dying person, to prepare for what is to come and to develop a foundation for future memories and legacies. For example, providing time for the child or adolescent to visit the dying person or allowing the youngster to offer gifts to the adult can be helpful for later grief. Even when the child or adolescent cannot or chooses not to carry through with a personal contact, tapes, phone calls, videos or other links may provide a symbolic presence.

Mode of Death and Concurrent Circumstances

Understanding Mode of Death and Concurrent Circumstances

Deaths that are "off time" are likely to present the most difficult challenges to survivors. Such deaths include those that are sudden, unexpected, traumatic, and human-induced (e.g., accidents, homicides, and suicides), as well as those in which the dying process is drawn out. Long-term dying may involve a variety of significant stressors on family members and others who are drawn into processes of coping with the end stages of a life-threatening illness. These include the depletion of one's energies in caring for the dying person, as well as living through a series of crises and returns to health (e.g., with AIDS and its recurring opportunistic infections). Children and adolescents often find it difficult to cope with experiences involved in witnessing the disfigurement or deterioration of the individual (e.g., in some forms of facial cancer), loss of functional capacities (e.g., in neurological diseases such as Parkinson's disease or amyotrophic lateral sclerosis), and loss of personality prior to physical death (e.g., in Alzheimer's disease).

Within a family system there may be important issues for children and adolescents associated with redistribution of the ill or dying person's roles to other members. There are special problems for children and adolescents when they are excluded from important events involving a family member, required to put their own needs aside in favor of those of others or asked to take on new burdens that may sometimes exceed their developmental capacities. Each long-term illness has its own dynamics, and each individual or family system is likely to live out its challenges in particular ways. But for children and adolescents, there are often issues such as those related to responsibility (Did I cause Grandpa's cancer?), blame (Did Uncle Ted's AIDS result from his life style?), and guilt (Did I wish my father would get it over with and die so that the rest of us could go back to our normal life?).

It is important to add that, even in cases of long-term dying, children and adolescents who have been excluded from or who do not normally have close contact with the dying person may perceive the death to have taken place rather quickly. In some families a child or adolescent may experience multiple illnesses, losses and deaths within a relatively short time. In these "dying families," a youngster who is not personally ill may be forced to struggle with a heavy burden of challenges associated with life-threatening illnesses, such as those related to HIV-infection and the deaths of more than one family member. In addition, a grieving child or adolescent may simultaneously be contending with such stressors as abusive or inadequate parenting at home, poverty in the neighborhood, violence at school, and dislocations involved in foster care or institutionalization.

Helping with Mode of Death and Concurrent Circumstances

For adult helpers, it is important to explore with a grieving child or adolescent his or her knowledge of and concerns about the illness or mode of death of a loved one. Begin with active listening and empathetic inquiry focusing on what the youngster has been told about the dying or death of a loved one and what are his or her main concerns.

A helping interaction might continue by: providing accurate information about the illness or mode of death and its related circumstances; dispelling misinformation and myths; working with parents and other family members to mobilize family values and develop frameworks that help a bereaved child or adolescent make sense out of or find meaning in the death; facilitating the identification of strong feelings and other reactions to the encounter and venting them in constructive ways; and working with the youngster to develop and implement appropriate commemorative activities to memorialize the life of the person who has died.

At the same time, helpers can also work with bereaved children and adolescents to explore other events or aspects of their lives that may contribute to making the illness or death more or less difficult. Experiences such as being handed over to new caregivers, moved to a new neighborhood, transferred to a new school or asked to cope with a new parental figure in place of one who has died can all complicate the bereavement of a child or adolescent.

In short, helpers who approach a child or adolescent who is grieving a long-term illness or death will do well to explore the implications of the illness/dying process, the mode of death and the concurrent circumstances in the youngster's life in order to determine whether or not (and how) each of these have affected his or her grief and coping. Often the helper may work directly with the child; sometimes it may be sufficient to draw the attention of parents and other family members to the needs of the child or adolescent.

Coping Strategies

Understanding Coping Strategies

Some have claimed that bereaved children and adolescents do not have the capacity to cope with or mourn a death in their lives. That claim depends in part on assumptions about children's inability to understand the finality of death and in part on suppositions about what is involved in coping with or mourning a death. Claims such as these are often found to depend upon assumptions and suppositions drawn from research on adults. In fact, whether or not children and adolescents understand death in what are thought to be mature or adult ways, it is a commonly-observed fact that they often inquire about or try to understand many new events in their lives and that they make efforts of various sorts to manage events that they perceive as stressful.

This is *coping*: the constantly changing efforts to manage what one perceives to be stressful. When an illness or death is not perceived to be stressful, as when there was no significant prior attachment to the deceased, there may be no need for coping. Routine, habitualized behaviors will be sufficient for everyday living. However, when an illness or death is perceived as stressful, a child or adolescent may attempt to manage its impact in a variety of ways— through play or sports, crying or clinging, or turning away from the harsh reality.

Fox (1988) suggested that in order to insure that the "grief work" of children and adolescents who are coping with death is in fact "good grief," it is helpful to conceptualize this in terms of four tasks:

1. to understand and begin to make sense out of what has happened;
2. to identify, validate, and express in constructive ways strong reactions to the loss;
3. to commemorate the life that was lived; and
4. to learn to go on with living and loving.

One could develop a task-based perspective of this sort in various ways. But the main point is the value of paying attention to the coping strategies and tasks of bereaved children and adolescents as they were before the beginning of the illness or dying process, during a trajectory of long-term dying and after a death.

Helping with Coping Strategies

Katzenbach (1986) indicated why grieving youngsters turn to adults for help in coping when he wrote that:

> Children can adapt wonderfully to specific fears, like a pain, a sickness, or a death. It is the unknown which is truly terrifying for them. They have no fund of knowledge in how the world operates, and so they feel completely vulnerable (p. 322).

Adults who wish to offer to grieving children and adolescents the benefits of their experiences and insights should explore two main points. What are the important sources of stress for the child's or adolescent's grief? And how can the child or adolescent best be helped to improve his or her coping with those sources of stress?

With respect to sources of stress, much will relate to the challenges to, or ending of, the attachment, the mode of death, and concurrent circumstances. With respect to ways in which the child or adolescent is coping, one can explore how the youngster has coped with stressful situations in the past, who his or her role models in coping have been, and what he or she has learned about coping. Individuals such as parents and other respected adults, society in general, and the child's own life experiences are likely to have been the source of situations that called for coping responses.

Adults and society often communicate spoken or unspoken guidelines about what are regarded as appropriate or inappropriate coping responses. Helpers are unlikely to effect major changes in a child or adolescent's coping strategies, even within the extended time frames of long-term illness and dying or in their aftermath. Nevertheless, understanding how and why the youngster has coped and is coping can guide the helper in interactions with the child or adolescent. From this foundation, helpers can assist significant adults to help a child or adolescent with his or her coping. All who are helping can work to model, teach, and develop constructive coping tactics.

Small improvements in coping with loss and grief, both before and after a prolonged illness or death, may lead to immediate and long-term benefits in the well-being of a bereaved child or adolescent.

Developmental Situation

Understanding Developmental Situations

All human beings face normative or predictable tasks in the course of their life-long development. These tasks have been conceptualized by Erik Erikson (and many others) in terms of various eras within the life span, predominant psychosocial challenges or conflicts within each era, and "leading virtues"—strengths or qualities of ego functioning that result from successful coping with each set of challenges (see Table 1). Appreciation of this developmental background is of great value in understanding grieving children and adolescents.

What long-term illness and death add to this are non-normative or specific situational challenges that may interrupt or complicate the work of normative development in childhood and adolescence. For example, opportunistic infections associated with HIV infection may render a mother unable to provide consistent and nurturing support for her infant. As a result, the infant may be unable to develop trust in his or her environment and may exhibit anxiety and a sense of insecurity both in the first year of life and thereafter. Similarly, a preschool child may become confused and guilt-ridden if he or she assumes responsibility for the erratic and difficult behavior of a grandparent with Alzheimer's disease. Such a child may not know how to take action to address this misplaced sense of responsibility and may be left unclear about purposeful initiatives in his or her life.

Situational challenges associated with long-term illness, dying, and death of a significant adult may also disrupt development during the adolescent years. For example, an early adolescent focusing on decreased identification with parents, as well as increased identification with peers, fascination with hero figures and interest in opposite-sex peers, may find it difficult to cope with an elderly parent who seems to be withdrawing or separating from the teen as a result of a progressive neurological disease. Likewise, a middle or late adolescent pursuing intimacy and enriched relationships with his or her parents may find these difficult to achieve when one parent dies of cancer, the other remarries within six months and a new step-parent, and possibly that individual's natural children, come onto the scene.

The issue in all of this is how children and adolescents understand, cope with, and integrate loss, death, and grief into their lives. In terms of understanding, it is common for adults to assume that younger children have no concept of death and that a mature concept of death is only achieved in a stage-like progression of children's cognitive capacities (Corr, 1995). There is much in this that is oversimplified and questionable. A more practical approach may be to ask questions like: What is the child able to understand? What does the child want to understand? What does the child need to understand? (Doka, 1996). With regard to coping with long-term illness, dying and death, questions like the following are likely to take center stage in early and middle childhood: Did I cause it? Can I catch it? Who will take care of me? In short, efforts to understand the grief of a child or adolescent need to take into account the developmental situation of the individual youngster.

Helping with Developmental Situations

A useful beginning for helping grieving children and adolescents with developmental situations can be made from the realization that "death is one of the central themes in human development throughout the life span. Death is not just our destination; it is a part of our 'getting there' as well" (Kastenbaum, 1977, p. 43). Childhood and adolescence are not periods in which death and loss are simply absent from human experience. Blissful innocence is a fantasy of adult projections. This means that helpers must begin with a sensitivity to the developmental realities of a particular child or adolescent who is grieving. The question to ask is how death has become a distinctive part of that child or adolescent's "getting there." That is, how have long-term illness, dying, or death affected the youngster's development, and in what ways have developmental capacities hindered or facilitated the youngster's abilities to cope with these situational challenges.

To do this, helpers must be sensitive to the full range of human development (not just cognitive or affective dimensions), listen to the individual child or adolescent, recognize the influence of his or her life experiences, and pay close attention to his or her modes of communication.

From a broader standpoint, in cases of long-term illness or dying, helpers should be alert to developmental changes in the child or adolescent during the illness/dying process or after the death. From an even more extended point of view, helpers will want to recognize and help the particular child or adolescent appreciate that issues associated with development in later life may reactivate old or unfinished grieving. For example, a child whose grandparent died during his or her preschool years may feel that loss keenly in elementary school when other children make cards or draw pictures on Grandparents' Day, just as an early adolescent may pine for guidance and reassurance from a long-dead parent when he or she begins dating.

Availability and Nature of Support

Understanding the Availability and Nature of Support

During a long-term illness or in the immediate aftermath of death, there may be little if anything that can be done to alter the prior attachment to the deceased, his or her mode of death, the concurrent circumstances of a bereaved child or adolescent or that child or adolescent's developmental situation. Some specific coping tactics may be changed or redirected in the near term, while broader coping strategies may be redesigned in more productive ways over the longer term. Limitations facing helpers are apparent with respect to each of these major factors that affect the grief of a child or adolescent.

By contrast, there is great latitude in the availability and nature of the support that is or may be offered to a bereaved child or adolescent. Questions to ask about availability might include: Is any support available to the bereaved child or adolescent? When is that support available? How is it offered? By whom? Sometimes the answers to these questions are that no support is available; that if available it is only offered in limited or unpredictable ways; that it is offered grudgingly or conditionally; or that the sources of such support are unclear or unreliable.

Related questions concern the nature of the support. Is it constructive and helpful? Or does it disenfranchise the loss ("your grandfather was already very old"), the grief ("he's better off now and you shouldn't be angry or sad that he's gone; instead, put a smile on your face and be strong"), or the griever ("children like you don't really understand death and don't have to worry about it for a long time")?

All too often, adults who are preoccupied by their own concerns or who have been drained of their energies by a long-term dying may not appreciate a grieving child or adolescent's need for support or may not be able to provide the support that is needed. This may also take place when the central loss, as in the personality of an Alzheimer's patient, occurs well before physical death. Or it may occur when the grief of a child extends over a long period of time but is only expressed or manifested intermittently.

Helping with Support

Helpers can do much to support grieving children and adolescents, both directly and indirectly. As concerned adults, they can themselves provide some of the support that may be needed by such a child or adolescent. As advocates working on behalf of the child or adolescent, they can call for assistance from parents and other adults, as well as formal or informal networks within other relatives, neighbors, schools, and communities. Where it seems appropriate (usually when the child or adolescent is having difficulty with activities of daily living and other age-appropriate behaviors), they can refer a grieving child or adolescent to a bereavement support group, an experienced grief counselor, or a competent grief therapist.

Many individuals and organizations can help grieving children and adolescents. Helpers might draw upon the special skills of art, music, and play therapists, as well as organizations with expertise related to children and adolescents, those which serve grieving youngsters and those who care for them or those mobilized around the diseases that lead to long-term illness and dying in our society. Beyond this, there is now available an extensive body of literature about bereavement in childhood and adolescence, as well as print and audiovisual resources for children, adolescents, and those who care for them (e.g., Corr and Balk, 1996; Corr and Corr, 1996).

Conclusion

Adults can do much to help grieving children and adolescents in cases of long-term illness, dying, and death. Understanding the impact of these encounters on grieving children and adolescents may be facilitated by attention to the five factors examined in this chapter:

1. the prior attachment to the ill, dying, or deceased person;
2. the mode of death and concurrent circumstances;
3. the coping strategies that the child or adolescent has learned to use in managing previous losses;
4. the developmental situation of the particular child or adolescent; and
5. the availability and nature of support.

Helping bereaved children and adolescents can also be guided by these same five factors. In truth, however, successful helping in most situations is primarily a matter of effective communication, prior education, validation of the youngster's needs, and caring support. Specific knowledge and professional skills are especially relevant to instances of complicated bereavement. In most other cases, helpers function best by honoring the youngster's grief, upholding the confidence that grieving children and adolescents have the natural capacity to cope with loss and grief, and trusting that difficult events in life can become opportunities for growth.

Table 1. Principal Developmental Eras in the Human Life Cycle

Era	Age*	Predominant Issue	Virtue
Infancy	birth through 12–18 months	Basic Trust vs. Mistrust	Hope
Toddlerhood	infancy to 3 years of age	Autonomy vs. Shame and Doubt	Will or Self-Control
Early Childhood; sometimes called Play Age or the Pre-School Period	3–6 years of age	Initiative vs. Guilt	Purpose or Direction
Middle Childhood; sometimes called School Age or the Latency Period	6 years to puberty	Industry vs. Inferiority	Competency
Adolescence	puberty to about 21 or 22 of age	Identity vs. Role Confusion	Fidelity
Young Adulthood	21–22 to 45 years of age	Intimacy vs. Isolation	Love
Middle Adulthood or Middle Age	45–65 years of age	Generativity vs. Stagnation and Self-Absorption	Production and Care
Maturity; sometimes called Old Age or the era of the Elderly	65 years of age and older	Ego Integrity vs. Despair	Renunciation and Wisdom

* Note: All chronological ages are approximate.
Source: Erikson, 1963, 1968.

A Decalogue: Ten Commandments for the Concerned Caregiver

11

Rabbi Earl A. Grollman, D.D.

Grieving is hard work—work that tears at you in so many ways. Grief taxes every part of you—body, soul and spirit. And when loss comes after a prolonged illness you may feel that you have twice as much work. And in many ways, you do—for you are grieving both during and after the illness.

There really are no commandments in grief. But I offer this decalogue, a list of ten recommendations, to help sustain your spirit as you grieve. For those of you who are not family members or friends, but formal caregivers—nurses, doctors, clergy, counselors—this decalogue is for you, too. Your calling is not only to minister in whatever way to the spirit of others—you also grieve, and you must sustain your spirit. Only by struggling with your own healing can you help others heal.

During the Prolonged Illness

I. Be Realistic

"I believe God creates miracles. No matter what the doctor says, he'll get better. You'll see."

A Jewish expression states: "Believe in miracles but be prepared for alternatives." William James said it differently: "Acceptance of what is truly happening is the first step to overcoming the consequences of misfortune."

Of course, you don't want to accept the diagnosis. You can't imagine that your loved one is so sick and will die. Feelings of vulnerability mount. Suddenly you realize that you are not in control. The truth is that no one is as powerful as he or she would like to think. And some miracles may not happen. When you cling to false expectations, you distort the present and postpone the future. Truth challenges you to understand what the human being is capable of enduring.

Think in terms of possibility—not impossibility. There will be moments when you want to believe that all is back to normal and that your prayers are being answered. Then an event takes place where actuality forces you into a downward plunge. Though reality is harsh and unfeeling, it is the compass which keeps you on track, a directional guide to aid you through your painful journey.

> If there is a sin against life, it consists not so much as despairing of life rather than in hoping for another.
> —Albert Camus

II. Be Informed

"I'm so confused. I know my loved one is seriously ill but I honestly don't completely understand what is really wrong with her and what I can do to help."

A natural coping mechanism of defense is to shut out potentially agonizing news. Yet to cope with adversity, you must speak with the health professionals to understand the impact of the illness and how you can be of the most assistance.

Before speaking to the doctors, organize your thoughts. Concentrate on the real concerns: diagnosis, prognosis, tests, treatments, procedures, research findings. Ask specific questions. Stay on track. Delve into important matters. Don't be embarrassed to share your real fears and anxieties. What really needs further clarification?

Concentrate. Actively focus your attention on what is being expressed. React to ideas, not to the person. Don't interrupt. And remember to listen. Your listening rate is faster than your speaking rate. (Speech rate is about 100 to 150 words per minute; thinking and listening is eight times as fast). It is you who must hear, understand and learn in order to help your loved one and yourself.

God in Hebrew is called *Rofé*, meaning healer. But says Ecclesiasticus: "Honor the physician whom the Lord hath appointed."

III. Be Caring of Your Physical Health

"How can I help my loved one when I'm so tired all the time?"

For of the soul, the body form doth take
For soul is form, and doth the body make.
—Spenser

Just as your heart aches, so does your body complain of severe loss of appetite, insomnia, fatigue. It is so draining to care for your loved one and yourself.

Walking can be an energizer. Adrenaline pumps through the body as you are revitalized, which can lead to feeling, eating, and sleeping better. As you move your feet, your mind begins to clear and the sinking feeling in the pit of the stomach may gradually begin to disappear.

You might benefit from extended activity, such as jogging, tennis, swimming, aerobics. Exercise produces powerful stress-reducing effects, fending off anxiety and depression, reducing risks of coronary mortality.

Be sure to check first with your physician. Then build your endurance gradually but surely. At this time of apprehension and stress, respect your body more than ever. You must maintain your health if you are to effectively take care of yourself and others.

IV. Be Caring of Your Emotional Health

"I feel so empty; life means nothing anymore."

The great object of life is sensation—to feel that we exist even in pain.
—Lord Byron

Caregiving is a high stress activity. Stress is a word borrowed from the field of engineering describing force applied to a structure. Stress also refers to the ordinary and extraordinary pressures of life. There are frequent ordinary pressures which you confront daily. Now there are new extraordinary stresses controlled by the unforeseen episodic nature of this devastating, prolonged illness.

You must take care of yourself in order to cope with this tragedy. Leave spaces in the day to find that deep and wordless place within you. In solitude you recharge your batteries. You nourish your mind—not drain it. Choose wisely, whether it be meditation, prayer, or quiet moments just for yourself. When you don't calm down and refresh yourself, life gets out of control. The peace that you find will make you a better caregiver.

> When from our better selves we have
> been too long parted by the hurrying
> world and droop—how gracious,
> how benign in solitude.
> —William Wordsworth

You might discover quiet moments of reflection, inspiration, and connectedness in nature. There is healing in experiencing a majestic sunrise, a peaceful lake, a star-studded sky. Sights and smells of the unity of earth afford warmth and comfort. Nature's grandeur brings peace of mind and helps to repair the wounds of loss.

When you are tense and troubled, fearful of the future, listening to music can create a soothing atmosphere, relieving anxiety, calming anguish and uncertainties. Science has demonstrated how music can actually lower the heart rate. That's why there are professional music therapists to help reach and comfort cares and restlessness. Soothing music interrupts negative thoughts and changes your emotional direction. A familiar melody might evoke pleasant memories, recent or remote. That's why music has been called The Great Healer, The Comforter, The Companion, The Medicine of the Breaking Heart.

V. Be Caring of Your Spiritual Health

Who can improve the prayer of Mother Theresa?

> Dearest Lord,
>
> May I see you today in the person of your sick, and while nursing them, minister to you. Give me faith so that my work will never be monotonous. O beloved sick, what a privilege is mine to be allowed to tend you!
>
> Lord, make me appreciative of the dignity of my high vocation. Never permit me to give way to coldness and hurry. Bless my work, now and forever more.

You will need to do the things that keep you spiritually in tune. Take time for spiritual care. Worship, walks, prayer, meditation, readings, or listening to music may be ways that you attend to your own spirituality. Despite the busyness, do not separate yourself from your sources of spiritual nourishment and strength. Now they are even more critical.

After the Death

VI. Don't Compare Deaths

> *"My friend kept telling me how fortunate I am. After all, my wife was sick for such a long time and I had time to be with her. Her husband was killed in a car accident and she had no opportunity to prepare for such a catastrophic event."*

Comparisons are odious and offer great grievances.
—Burton

It is different when someone dies accidentally or suddenly. The impact is profound. There is no forewarning. Survivors feel powerless after their overpowering shock. The assault on emotions makes it so difficult to believe and accept. One moment the world may seem fine; the next, the world crumples before their very eyes.

They may ask you: "Why are you taking it so hard? You *knew* she was dying. It's not as if you didn't have any warning. Didn't you have time to prepare for this?"

They don't understand. Whatever the circumstances, you are probably *never* prepared. Death almost always comes unexpectedly. Even after a prolonged illness, no one can completely plan for death. An old adage says: "If you want to make God laugh, tell Him of your plans."

It doesn't help when people say to you: "Thank God, her suffering is over." Your loved one's suffering may be over, but yours isn't. Don't allow others—or even yourself—to deny or camouflage your grief.

Yes, you knew how sick she was. Yet, you may be swept away by onrushing feelings. It's so difficult to have the link with your past severed completely. No matter how prolonged the illness, grief is still unbearable heartache, sorrow, loneliness. Because you loved, grief continues to walk by your side.

VII. Don't Feel Guilty If Your Feel a Sense of Relief

"I loved my daughter so much. She was so terribly sick for so long. Yet, now that she is dead, I sometimes feel so relieved that she's no longer in pain and I don't have to worry about her any more. I am free from any responsibility. But I feel so guilty when I say this."

For this relief much thanks. 'Tis bitter cold,
And I am sick at heart.
—Shakespeare

One emotion that may surprise you is relief. Perhaps her excruciating torment is over and she is at peace. Perhaps she depended upon you so much and now there is a sense of reprieve to know that you are no longer encumbered.

It is perfectly appropriate to feel relieved at the same time you are feeling devastated. The task of caring for a dying person is dreadfully difficult. Waves of relief come and go. These emotions are normal; you are not calloused and uncaring. You need not feel guilty. The prolonged illness is past and you have been released from an all-consuming task. Your feelings of relief are well earned.

VIII. Don't End Your Search for Finding Meaning in Loss

"I feel so useless, so helpless. If only I could do something to make my loved one's memory mean something to others."

Those who bring sunshine to others cannot keep it from themselves.
—Sir James Barrie

You, who have experienced grief, are better able to understand the grief of others. You can be a wounded healer reaching out to others who are experiencing similar circumstances. Sharing is healing, and you help when you share.

Reach out. In relating to others, you start to let go of that terrible emptiness in your own heart. You take the focus off yourself. You reinvest in others. Reaching out makes you feel needed, wanted, important. Others need your understanding and compassion. You are the expert; you have been there. You are not alone in undergoing pain and crisis. One touch of sorrow makes the whole world kin.

In Jewish literature, the Dubner Maggid has left us a parable whose wisdom can serve as a beacon of light for your dark days:

A king once owned a large, beautiful, pure diamond of which he was justifiably proud, for it had no equal anywhere. One day, the diamond accidentally sustained a deep scratch. The king called in the most skilled diamond cutters and offered them a great reward if they could remove the imperfection from the treasured jewel. But none could repair the blemish. The king was sorely distressed.

After some time, a gifted jeweler came to the king and promised to make the rare diamond even more beautiful than it had been before the mishap. The king was impressed by his confidence and entrusted the precious stone to his care.

With superb artistry, he engraved a lovely rosebud around the imperfection and he used the scratch to make the stem.

When a loved one dies and life's bruises wound you, you can use the scratches to etch a portrait of meaning and purpose for others. Through your own life, you will prolong their memories.

IX. Don't End Your Search for Growth and Purpose

"I hurt so much. Will I ever find peace?"

That which does not kill me makes me stronger.
—Fredrich Nietzche

Pain, loss and separation can lead you to growth, or they can destroy your life. Death brings you this choice. It can lead you to the edge of the abyss, but you can build a bridge that will span the chasm.

Now that you've encountered loss, you may see life differently. When someone you love dies, you confront your own mortality. Knowing how brief life can be might encourage you to try to make your own life more meaningful and enjoyable.

Now that you've encountered loss, you may be looking more deeply into your own beliefs. What had been significant may now appear trivial. You may set new priorities and redefine your needs. Growing is knowing not only where you have been, but what you are searching for.

Now that you've encountered loss, you may have a different understanding of the meaning of love. You realize that loving others doesn't diminish your love for the one who died. Love doesn't die; people do.

Grief begins with a terrible and lonely loss. Grief changes you but it is not destroying you. Grief is a powerful teacher.

"Who are You?" said the Caterpillar. Alice replied, rather shyly, "I hardly know, Sir, just at present—at least I know who I *was* when I got up this morning, but I think I must have been changed several times since then."

How different you are now. Nothing in life had prepared you for this tragedy. Like Alice, you have had to make many changes to adjust to your great loss.

Take small steps and take pride in your small victories. Your love for the person has made your life richer by what you have shared. Your growth in the midst of your pain can bear fruit in your spirit and make you all the richer.

X. Don't End Your Search for Spirituality

"Don't talk to me about faith. Where were you, God, when I desperately needed you? Why didn't you stop the illness before it began? You tell me to believe and trust. How can I?"

My eyes have grown dim with grief;
My whole frame is but a shadow.
—Job 17:7

Grief is not only physical, emotional, and social. It is also spiritual. Spirituality has been described as the art of "staying connected in a disconnected world." More than 250 studies demonstrate a positive link between spirituality and good mental health.

Dying and death is a journey into the unknown. There are questions that you may not have been prepared to delve into before you were confronted with the prolonged illness. Spirituality is something you may wish to use, not lose, with a wisdom that has nourished the souls of humankind for untold generations. And sorrow can be a spiritual pilgrimage.

Regardless of whether you have a religious affiliation or not, you may not be spared from a crisis of meaning. Lengthy sickness changes life's purposes. Death makes you question beliefs as you struggle for answers. Do prayer, a faith community, a belief in a world-to-come make sense? Can you find the inner strength of "staying connected in a disconnected world?" William Faulkner's spirituality was in evidence when he received the Nobel Prize for Literature: "I believe that man will not merely endure; he will prevail. He is immortal, not because he alone among creatures has an inexhaustible voice, but because he has a soul, a spirit capable of compassion and sacrifice and endurance."

Evidence in the mystery of light and life may be discovered in the mystery of darkness and death. You may find that no event separates you from an Absolute, however you define it. "I rise before day and cry for help. I have put my hope in Your word" (Psalm 19). You may no longer feel so alone and forsaken. You may feel forgiven for whatever you feel you did or did not do. You may feel comforted even when perplexed with unanswered, bewildering problems. You may have renewed strength to transform the memory of the dead to meaningful memorials for the living.

You might find consolation in prayer. Prayer need not involve words. The Trappist monk Thomas Merton said, "I pray by breathing." Through your devotions you may gain a feeling of genuineness, empathy and caring, a consciousness of the power of love and the interconnectedness of all creation.

Rituals may help you express personal feelings of loss and sorrow. Symbols have the capacity to touch not just on an intellectual level, but on behavioral, emotional, and spiritual levels as well. They are powerful events which can help heal deep wounds and affirm one's truest self. Rituals may alter a state of mind by bringing something buried deep in the subconscious out into the open. Rituals are not the path; they are the reminder that there *is* a path.

Being part of a faith community can be therapeutic. John Donne said so long ago, "No man is an island." You do not stand alone. Each person's joy is a joy to you and each person's grief is your own. In a community of faith, you come together because in being together you share the power of heritage, tradition, and spiritual beliefs. You begin to recenter yourself, enabling yourself to begin to make that painful transition from prolonged illness and death towards life.

As you seek spiritual responses to the profound issues of good and evil, you may begin to release feelings of helplessness and guilt and discover a measure of comfort, belonging and hope. Unfortunately, studies show that the spiritual concerns of dying people and their families are often overlooked in health care literature. In a holistic approach to death and dying, the patient must be viewed not only as a physical entity but as a whole person with biopsychological and spiritual needs as well. Spirituality may not take away heartache. But spirituality may help you to better live with adversity and to accept the unacceptable.

Meaning Reconstruction and the Experience of Chronic Loss

12

Robert A. Neimeyer, Ph.D.

U ntil she was 34, Kerry led what she had always considered a "charmed" life. Relatively affluent and outgoing, she had been popular among her peers through high school. In her early 20's, she married to begin the family she had always wanted. Even her divorce from what she later conceded to be a "premature" marriage did little to perturb a life filled with the external rewards of abundance and social belongingness. While she sometimes harbored inner doubts about having the "depth" and "love" she sometimes perceived in others, for the most part her life remained "easy and beautiful" as it progressed along a predictable course of social and community involvement. Her second marriage, to her college sweetheart, seemed to confirm the "normality" of her life, as she gave birth to a healthy daughter, and a few years later, conceived a son.

Then, with the birth of her son, Jacob, all this changed. For the next two years Kerry found herself the primary caretaker to an infant with a congenital heart defect, alternately embracing and resenting the heavy burden of constant vigilance and sacrifice. Every few weeks

Note: Portions of this chapter appear in Neimeyer, R.A, Keesee, N.J. and Fortner, B.V. (1997). "Loss and meaning reconstruction: Propositions and procedures." In S. Rubin, R. Malkinson and E. Wiztum (Eds.). *Traumatic and Non-traumatic Loss and Bereavement: Clinical theory and practice*. Madison, CT: Psychosocial Press.

for the two years her son lived, Kerry would detect further symptoms of heart failure in Jacob and accompany him to the hospital, praying that some miracle would be performed or some medication administered that would allow her to return to the normal life she craved. But night after night, as she lay sleepless and crying on a cot in her son's hospital room, she found these prayers unanswered. Even with the occasional support of friends and family, she felt trapped in an exhausting and emotionally-draining existence, displaced from the people, patterns and projects that had once given her life a familiar form. When Jacob died during the last of these lengthy hospitalizations, Kerry felt disoriented and inconsolable, and struggled for an answer for what it had all meant, both for herself and her family. She found no easy answers.

• • •

At age 76, Clara had built a life on self-sacrifice. The third of four children in a conservative Jewish family, Clara learned and internalized the historical suffering of her people and came to view devotion to one's purpose and loyalty to others as the guiding principles of life. As a young woman, she had entered the nursing profession, working in an environment that frequently demanded that she place her own needs behind those of others. Clara's personal life reinforced these patterns, as she devoted herself to raising three children without the support of her workaholic husband, while simultaneously providing in-home care for his mother during the years of slow deterioration leading to her death.

Then, in late life, Clara faced a dilemma for which she could find no solution. Her husband, Ed, lay "dying by degrees" in a nursing home, having suffered a series of strokes that left him disabled and noncommunicative much of the time. Perhaps the only constant in his personality was his anger and combativeness. Long abusive to Clara both emotionally and physically, he now fluctuated between crying like a small child and raging wildly at perceived injustices by both the nursing home staff and Clara herself. Clara left these daily visits feeling "tortured and depressed," to the point of contemplating suicide as the only way out of what she saw as the insoluble "trap" of the need to care for a man who alternately begged for and rejected her attempts at caretaking. To complicate her situation, Clara's oldest son, Richard, had become increasingly forceful in demanding that she discontinue her painful visits to a father he had resented all his life. Unable to behave in so "selfish" a manner, Clara now began to feel estranged from the son who loved her most, as well from the helpless husband who apparently hated her.

• • •

As we strive to understand the many forms of chronic loss and their impact on survivors, we are quickly pushed to the limits of our conventional models of grief and bereavement. As human beings struggling with seemingly inhuman demands, we all too often find ourselves caricatured in the overly simple portrayal of grief offered by traditional "stage" theories of adaptation to loss. Not only do these theories seem strangely anonymous, but they also seem to miss the particulars of our struggle. They do not seem rooted in our own unique life. As I have tried across time to come to terms with the losses in my own life and in the lives of those I have counseled, I have questioned the adequacy of conventional understandings of grief. These efforts have gradually led me to an alternative view, one that is shared by a small but growing group of clinicians, theorists, and researchers concerned with bereavement. This view, which resonates with what has been termed a *constructivist* approach to psychotherapy (Neimeyer and Mahoney, 1995), takes as its fundamental assumption that the attempt to reconstruct a world of meaning is the central process in the experience of grieving. In this chapter, I will sketch a few propositions drawn from this view, using the particulars of Kerry's and Clara's cases to illustrate its implications for our work with those who are engaged in this process.

Traditional Models of Grief and Their Limitations

A common denominator of most traditional theories of grief is their identification of a series of stages or phases of adjustment, beginning with the actual or imminent death of a loved one and progressing through various forms of emotional reaction, until the bereaved individual achieves some form of recovery or reconciliation. While these models of mourning can be traced at least to the work of Lindemann (1944), who divided grief into the stages of shock-disbelief, acute mourning and resolution, the most influential of these theories is that proposed by Kubler-Ross (1969). The focus of her work was the emotional transition—beginning with denial and progressing through anger, bargaining and depression, before ending in possible acceptance—experienced by terminal patients anticipating their own deaths; it has since been generalized (perhaps inappropriately) to a model of the grief process among survivors as well. Most subsequent stage models of bereavement have drawn upon some combination or variation of these two sequences, as in Engel's (1964) depiction of grief as involving phases of shock and disbelief, developing awareness, restitution, resolving the loss, idealization and outcome, or Canine's (1990) segmenting of the experience into periods of denial, numbness, searching, disorientation and resolution. One indication of the influence of this concept of loss is its privileged place in international medical school curricula on death and dying: Kubler-Ross's model is by far the most common resource (typically the only resource) cited by faculty members teaching residents about adaptation to death and loss (Downe-Wambolt and Tamlyn, 1997).

While some support for a stage theory of mourning can be derived from comparative developmental research on loss (Bowlby, 1980), most research on grieving has failed to find evidence for the validity and reliability of such a model (e.g., Corr, 1993; Feigenberg, 1980; Shneidman, 1980). While opening the door for discussion of death-related issues, these theories have found little empirical support for the presence of distinct psychological stages, much less for a determined sequence of psychological states (Davidson, 1979; Wortman and Silver, 1989). Following loss, many people do not demonstrate the proposed states at all or do not experience them in an identifiable sequence. Instead, the particular form of response, and the sequence and duration of emotional reactions to loss, vary greatly.

The lack of empirical evidence to support stage models, as well as my clinical observations and personal experience with loss, have led me to reject many of the implicit assumptions of traditional grief theories and to turn away from some of the clinical practices derived from such assumptions. I no longer assume that people experience a universal sequence of stages or tasks following loss or that the process of grieving can be viewed as ending in "recovery." I do not believe that the bereaved passively negotiate a train of psychological transitions forced upon them by external events. I cannot endorse the implication that a normative pattern of grieving can be prescriptive or diagnostic, and that deviations from such a course are to be considered "abnormal" or "pathological." More subtly, I question whether emotional responses should be considered the primary focus of our grief theories, to the exclusion or minimization of behavior and meaning. And finally, I have doubts about the individualistic bias of traditional theories of bereavement, which tend to construe grief as an entirely private act, experienced outside the context of human relatedness. All of these concerns have prompted an alternative model of grieving, predicated on a constructivist or narrative theory of meaning reconstruction in the wake of significant loss (Neimeyer, Keesee and Fortner, 1997; Neimeyer and Stewart, 1996). After outlining some of the criteria for such a theory, I will offer a few "working notes" in support of its assumptive structure, considering its relevance for grief therapy and grief counseling along the way.

Design Criteria for a Useful Grief Theory

From a constructivist perspective, a useful theory of grief would need to meet a number of criteria that stand in contrast to traditional theories. First, it would reveal the personal reality of death or loss for different individuals, instead of assuming that death holds a universal significance for human beings irrespective of their historical, cultural, familial or personal contexts. Rather than forcing individuals into a singular mold, it would be flexible enough to illuminate highly individual constructions of death and their changes over time. Second, it would view people as active in facing death's challenges rather than being passive reactors. In practical terms, our models of loss should sensitize us to the varied ways in which individuals and groups anticipate loss and assimilate it into personal and shared systems of belief. Third, the theory should be richly descriptive in elucidating personal meanings of loss, without subtly prescribing what constitutes "normal" grieving. It should allow the counselor or therapist to explore the limitations and entailments of any particular construction of loss, without idealizing or pathologizing its distinctive form or structure. Fourth, it would focus on passionately-held meanings that shape emotional, behavioral and physical responses. Thus, rather than viewing grief solely in terms of the emotional effects of loss, it would provide a more holistic depiction of adaptation to bereavement. Fifth, it would describe how one's world is forever transformed by loss rather than suggesting a return to some pre-morbid state following a "recovery." By extension, our models should permit us to trace changes in the bereaved individual's self and life that do not simply reduce to a reestablishment of pre-loss patterns. Finally, while maintaining a focus on the highly personal qualities of grief, a useful theory would allow for the consideration of grief in larger social and family contexts. Let us now turn to several propositions that my colleagues and I have found useful in developing our research and clinical practice (Neimeyer, Keesee and Fortner, 1997), and which we hope will contribute to a more comprehensive theory of grieving conceived along constructivist lines.

A Propositional Beginning

As a relatively recent addition to clinical practice, *constructivism* views human beings as meaning-makers, striving to punctuate, organize and anticipate their engagement with the world by construing it in themes that express their particular cultures, families and personalities (Mahoney, 1991; Neimeyer, 1987; 1995a). At an individual level, this suggests that persons construct systems of meaning, organized around a set of core assumptions, which both govern their perception of life events and channel their behavior in relation to them (Kelly, 1955). However, in contrast to more rationalistic cognitive theories that regard such interpretations as "irrational" or "dysfunctional" to the extent that they fail to mirror "objective" reality, constructivism suggests that human beings have no simple recourse to a reality beyond their grasp, and instead must judge the viability of their constructions on the basis of their practical utility, their internal coherence and their degree of consensual validation by relevant others (Neimeyer, 1993a; 1995b; Polkinghorne, 1992). One implication of this view is that any given "objective" event (such as loss) can be construed in many different ways, none of which is inherently valid or invalid, functional or dysfunctional.

Adopting this position as a starting point for a theory of loss suggests several propositions, which collectively begin to sketch an alternative framework for understanding the adaptive processes of grieving. I recognize that other grief theorists have also found traditional theories wanting (e.g., Attig, 1996; Doka and Morgan, 1993; Janoff-Bulman, 1992; Klass, Silverman and Nickman, 1996; Rubin, 1993; Worden, 1991), and have begun to work toward more adequate models of mourning that share features with the approach outlined here. I therefore will draw attention to the work of other authors that dovetails with our own and that helps provide a conceptual platform for designing new principles and procedures for the practice of grief therapy.

As a starting point for our work, we have outlined six straightforward propositions that are compatible with a constructivist position, and that together offer a fresh vantage point from which to view human mortality and bereavement (Neimeyer, Keesee and Fortner, 1997).

1. Death as an event can validate or invalidate the constructions that form the basis on which we live, or it may stand as a novel experience for which we have no constructions.

If we view human beings as constructing a unique world of meaning, then we need to understand the ways in which death can enter that world, confirming or denying those constructions that give human lives their direction. In the course of daily living, each of us is sustained by the network of habitual explanations, enactments and expectations that shape our lives with others. These tacit assumptions provide us with a basic sense of order regarding our past, familiarity regarding our current relationships, and predictability regarding our future. Experiences of loss that fit the contours of our constructions—as in the "appropriate" death of an elderly relative after a life well-lived, or the "heroic" death of a warrior who martyrs himself for a cause we passionately support—can provide powerful support for our assumptions about the world. But deaths that are discrepant with our core constructions—e.g., the suicide of a loved one or the chronic suffering and death of a spouse or child—can challenge the adequacy of our most cherished beliefs. In the latter case, the degree of reconstruction of our patterns of interpreting, anticipating and organizing our lives may be profound, and may never be fully accomplished. What is crucial is the extent to which a particular form of death or loss corresponds with our current ways of integrating experience, rather than the objective characteristics of the death itself. By implication, it is misleading to describe particular forms of death (e.g., violent, sudden) as inherently traumatic for survivors, except insofar as they are radically at odds with the constructions of that individual, family, or community.

In emphasizing the degree to which death supports or challenges our preexisting constructions of life, we are building upon the work of theorists such as Parkes (1988), who defined our assumptive worlds as the "internal models" against which we match incoming data in order to orient the self, recognize what is happening, and plan behavior. While this "information processing" interpretation may suggest that human beings operate in a highly cognitive and self-aware fashion, Rando (1995) clarifies that most of our assumptions "translate into virtually automatic habits of cognition and behavior," such that we might be quite unaware of the implicit expectations that we attach to a given relationship until we lose it.

Some valuable research associates traumatic loss with disruptions of general schemas for interpreting life events—e.g., viewing the world as benevolent, life as meaningful, and the self as worthy (Janoff-Bulman, 1989). However, it may actually be equally revealing to reverse this emphasis, and to consider the extent to which distinctive ways of interpreting loss can mitigate or exacerbate its impact. For example, qualitative research by Braun and Berg (1994) has found that grief adjustment was better for mothers who could assimilate the deaths of their children into an existing philosophical or spiritual belief system, just as Milo (1997) found that mothers who lost developmentally disabled children following chronic illness coped better when they could find personal significance in their children's lives, suffering and deaths. Such research underscores our emphasis on the extent to which a particular loss can either be given meaning within the framework of one's existing constructions, or can appear to actually undermine this very framework.

Despite its strengths, research on the assumptive world of grievers often lacks attention to meaning-making activity at a highly personal level, a level not easily reduced to a general search for an image of the world as just, the self as worthy, and life events as meaningful. For example, Jacob's protracted illness and death invalidated Kerry's view of life as something that was relatively easy and abundant, confronting her month after month with painful evidence that her previous way of living was inadequate to her current challenges. Not only did her philosophy of life leave her unprepared for the tragic complications of her son's congenital illness, but his death also triggered a profound re-evaluation of her priorities, her relationships, and even her sense of herself as a person.

2. Grief is a personal process, one that is idiosyncratic, intimate, and inextricable from our sense of who we are.

Grief can only be fully understood in the context of the everyday process of constructing, maintaining, and changing our most basic sense of self. Our personalities, outlooks and dispositions are determined neither by our genes nor our environment, but by our own investment in those persons, places and projects to which we are bound by bonds of caring attachment (Attig, 1996). We organize our identities as we go along, consolidating a sense of self and world by building personal theories or interpretations of our experiences. When events shake our sense of self and world, we respond by trying to interpret them in ways consistent with our overall theories and identities. When our most basic sense of self is assaulted, we lose our secure grip on familiar reality and are forced to reestablish another.

This proposition carries several implications for our conceptualization of grief and our assessment of its impact on individuals. To the extent that grief is shaped by these deeply personal processes of meaning making, it may be difficult to capture in common language. It may be especially hard to translate such disruption into standard "clinical" terminology or the rigid language of stages. This presents caregivers with a challenge to tune in to the more individual and intimate meanings of loss, forcing us to move beyond cliched expressions of support or preconceived ideas of what a particular loss "feels like" to any given griever. Instead, a deepened appreciation of the particularity of loss compels us to listen intently for clues to the uniqueness of bereavement for each client, which might best be conveyed in metaphors or imagery. The intimacy required to explore and name the multiple losses associated with any given death must be earned rather than assumed, and premature attempts to offer a clinical diagnosis or even helpful advice will typically distance us as caregivers from the griever's experience. Most basically, we need to appreciate more deeply the extent to which losses of those we love (or even those we hate) cause profound shifts in our sense of who we are, because no one else will ever occupy the unique position in relation to us that calls forth the parts of our past that were shared with the deceased person (Sluzki, 1991). In this sense, grieving entails not only a process of relearning a world disrupted by loss, but relearning the self as well (Attig, 1996).

Some of the intricacy of this process is suggested by Clara's attempt to come to terms with the chronic disability and impending death of her husband. Having constructed an identity based on a lifetime of selfless giving to others, she found herself unable either to resolve decades of unfinished business with Ed in the final months of his life, or to redefine her relationship with him. The same meaning system that had enabled her to survive the adversity of her earlier years now seemed to constrain her from living with some sense of acceptance and peace late in life. Empathically grasping and communicating this dilemma provided me with an entry point into her world of meaning and enabled me to explore alternative symbolic ways of "finishing the conversation" with Ed, and allowed her to affirm her core identity by redirecting her caring toward others.

3. Grieving is something we do, not something that is done to us.

Clearly, bereavement as such is a "choiceless event." We experience it as an unwelcome intruder in our lives, one who refuses to retreat despite our impassioned protests. The enormity of death can leave us feeling helpless and overwhelmed, and we may experience ourselves as pawns in a cosmic game that eludes our best attempts at understanding.

And yet, the experience of grieving itself may be rich in choice. At the most basic level we have a choice of whether to attend to the distress occasioned by our loss, to feel and explore the grief of our loved one's absence, or to disattend to or suppress our private pain and focus instead on adaptation to a changed external reality. This vacillation between engaging versus avoiding intensive "grief work" is fundamental to the "dual process" model of grieving proposed by Margaret Stroebe (1992), and may help account for the wide variation in mourning behavior found in different cultures (Stroebe and Stroebe, 1994).

At a more specific level, grieving involves hundreds of concrete choices, including whether to absorb the burden of caring for an ailing loved one or distribute it to others, whether to view the body of the deceased, whether to keep or dispose of the loved one's possessions, whether to continue to live in a home once shared with the one who has died, how and with whom to share one's account of the loss, whether to ritualize the death and if so in what fashion, and how to continue to relate to one's internal representation or "spirit" of the lost loved one (Attig, 1991). Thus, far from representing a passive process of experiencing a series of predictable emotional transitions, grieving needs to be seen more realistically as a period of accelerated decisionmaking on both existential and practical levels, to the point that the bereaved individual may feel overwhelmed by the challenges posed. Conceiving of grief as an intensely active process is valuable to us not only because it seems to correspond more closely to the experience of actual grievers, but also because it gives more potential direction to grief therapists, who can help to sensitize clients to the many subtle decisions they face, and help them sift through the implications of their conscious and unconscious choices.

Clara's predicament illustrates the paradoxical nature of choice and the necessarily active process of accommodating to loss. As an objective reality, Ed's illness was clearly not consciously "chosen" by Clara, although at a less conscious level she may have sometimes found herself wishing for his death during his abusive marriage to her. But now, faced with his post-stroke disability, she was confronted by choices that overwhelmed her. Should she have him transferred to a Jewish nursing home, threatening her increasingly tenuous financial stability, or continue to have him cared for in a secular facility and risk the approbation of her family and synagogue? Should she listen to the urgings of her son and stop "torturing herself" by visiting her dying but belligerent husband, or remain true to her marital vows to be with Ed until "death do us part?" Perhaps most urgently, should she—and could she—manage to somehow go on living in the face of such dilemmas, or take the "coward's way out" by ending her own life, even at the cost of bringing shame to her family? Much of the work of therapy consisted of looking at these questions in such a way that they could lead to more optimistic answers and permit her to focus on the less paralyzing process of reconstructing a life for herself following her husband's death.

4. Grieving is the act of affirming or reconstructing a personal world of meaning that has been challenged by loss.

To the extent that loss invalidates the assumptive structure of our lives in highly individualistic ways, challenging us to cope adaptively with a tumult of subjective experiences and objective demands, it requires us to reconstruct a world that again makes sense, that restores a semblance of meaning and direction to a life that is forever transformed.

A narrative model is helpful in understanding this process of meaning reconstruction, which we regard as the central dynamic of grieving. If life is viewed as a story (cf. Howard, 1991; Polkinghorne, 1991), then loss can be viewed as disrupting the continuity of the narrative. Like a novel that loses a central supporting character in a middle chapter, the life disrupted by bereavement forces its "author" to envision far-reaching plot changes in order for the story to move forward in an intelligible fashion. Moreover, chronic and protracted losses may gradually erode the plot structure of the "text" of one's biography, requiring continual revisions in the direction of one's life narrative, just at the point that we as authors have found a point of tenuous predictability. Constructing a way of bridging the past with a changing and uncertain future can be a major task, one that may require therapeutic support.

While complicated losses may dislocate us from the broader narrative of our lives, adaptive processes of reconstruction are also possible (Viney, 1991). On the one hand, we can assimilate loss into preexisting frameworks of meaning, ultimately reaffirming the viability of the belief system that previously sustained us, or we can accommodate our life narrative to correspond to a changed reality. The bereaved individual who integrates the protracted and painful death of a spouse into a long-held religious view emphasizing divine providence illustrates the former assimilative process, whereas the mourner who jettisons, revises or deepens his or her prior convictions exemplifies the latter accommodative process. Both movements may be adaptive in the sense that they reaffirm or reestablish a broad narrative structure in which tragedy is given personal meaning.

Assimilative processes of meaning making are most evident in the case of Clara, who approached her husband's tempestuous dying by integrating it into the same system that had served her for as long as she could remember. Thus, she attempted to deal with it as yet another form of hardship to be endured loyally, selflessly "being there" for another at the expense of her own needs. However, this well-practiced construction of her role seemed inadequate in the face of the emotional demands of caring for and witnessing the progressive demise of a man she loved, but also powerfully resented. Kerry, in contrast, recognized more and more clearly with each month of her son's illness that the previous structure of her life was inadequate to the task of interpreting, much less giving meaningful direction to, the alien world in which she now found herself. Casting about for explanations for her family's suffering, she came to see it as a God-given chance to atone for her own "unconsciousness," to live with greater self-awareness than she had in the past. In accepting this challenge, Kerry turned away from many of the trivial preoccupations that had once characterized her existence and began to reorder her relationships and priorities in a way that accorded with her new sense of self. Significantly for both women, their eventual reorganization was ushered in by a profound dislocation from their previous construction of life, precipitating a painful self-examination that led to a new, albeit fragile order.

Construing bereavement in narrative terms is more than a metaphor; it carries concrete, helpful implications for how grieving can be viewed and facilitated in a therapeutic context. At the most general level, a narrative view emphasizes "account-making," the way in which we tell and retell the stories of our loss, and in so doing, recruit social validation for the changed story lines of our lives (Harvey, 1996). More specifically, it suggests several "narrative means to therapeutic ends" (White and Epston, 1990), including the clinical use of specially-adapted forms of journaling, poetic writing, or other expressive therapies to help consolidate the implications of loss and integrate them more completely into our lives (Neimeyer, 1995c; Neimeyer and Stewart, 1996). In this way constructivism provides not only specific techniques to facilitate meaning making, but also a framework within which they can be used in grief therapy or counseling.

5. Feelings have functions and should be understood as signals of the state of our meaning-making efforts.

Ironically, despite the emphasis of traditional grief theories on the emotional effects of bereavement, affective grief responses are typically treated as merely problems to be overcome with the passage of time or "treatment." In contrast to this, constructivists view emotions as integral to meaning making, as expressions of our efforts to grasp a changed "reality" (Kelly, 1955; Mahoney, 1991). Feelings have a function, and are to be respected as integral to the process of meaning reconstruction, rather than controlled or eliminated as unwanted by-products of the loss itself (Neimeyer, 1993).

Drawing on a personal construct view of emotions as "dimensions of transition" (Kelly, 1955), I have found it useful to reconceptualize many of the emotional experiences of bereavement in terms that link them with the disruption or restoration of our meaning-making efforts. Denial is understood as one's inability to assimilate a death at a given point in time. One does not have recourse to the structure necessary to fully perceive the loss or its implications. Denial therefore represents an attempt to "suspend" the event for a time, until its meaning can be grasped in all its painful clarity. Depression can be viewed as a bereaved individual's attempt to restrict his or her focus to fewer and fewer concerns in order to render the world more manageable. Like a frightened child hiding under a bed during a thunderstorm, the depressed individual can be seen as constricting his or her experiential world to defend against further potential invalidation and to focus attention on sifting through the multiple meanings of the loss. Anxiety represents the awareness that the death lies largely outside one's ability to explain, predict and control. The fact of death or loss is clearly perceived, but we remain only dimly aware of its unsettling implications for our future lives. Guilt stems from the perception that one has behaved in a way that contradicts one's central structures of identity. As such, it is a personal, rather than social, assigning of culpability for having failed to live up to self-imposed standards for one's role in relationship to others. Hostility can be viewed as the attempt to force events to conform to our constructions of them, extorting evidence that validates our failed predictions. In this sense, we hostilely impose our own interpretations on a death event when we force it to fit with the constructions we held prior to the loss, regardless of whether it fits this structure. And, finally, threat signals the awareness of impending comprehensive change in core identity structures. A particular form of death or loss may portend sweeping changes in our most basic sense of who we are.

While this list of emotional transitions associated with loss is a preliminary one, I find it useful in orienting us to the possible meanings of common feelings and stances that characterize bereavement. For example, Clara's depression can be understood as a form of constriction of her experiential world, to the point that she was preoccupied almost totally with her role in relation to her dying husband. While this focus on his suffering and her unresolved relationship with him was painful, it can also be seen as being adaptive, insofar as it allowed her to shift the focus away from other anxiety-producing areas of her life—such as the expectations of others and the necessary reorganization of her life in the wake of his eventual death. Clara also contended with a heavy feeling of guilt whenever she withdrew even for a day from her core role as Ed's selfless caregiver. In contrast, Kerry's initial emotional experience during her son's long dying trajectory was one of denial, as she tried vainly to maintain the hope that he would recover and lead a normal life. As the anguishing reality became apparent, however, she undertook a thorough revision of her meaning system in line with her cosmological explanation of the event, transforming herself and her values in the process. While this way of looking at emotions in meaning-making terms is useful in promoting a fuller understanding of individual cases like these, it has also been helpful in suggesting novel ways of measuring death attitudes in research settings, as represented in the extensive program of study on death threat conducted by personal construct investigators (Neimeyer, 1994).

6. We construct and reconstruct our identities as survivors of loss in negotiation with others.

Too often, grief theories isolate the bereaved person, focusing so exclusively on the reactions of the individual suffering loss that his or her connection to others is ignored. While I also believe that a useful grief theory must account for the personal nature of loss, I find that adjustment to loss can ultimately be understood only in a broader social context. For this reason, I envision "grief work" as being done at the level of three interdependent and nested systems, of the self, family, and broader society.

At the level of the self, the individual can be viewed as a constellation or community of semi-autonomous "selves" (Mair, 1977), each of which is supported by certain relationships and each of which might respond to death or loss in different ways. Adopting a metaphor of the self as a complex system of personalities, coping capacities, beliefs and so on offers greater clinical utility than traditional theories of personality that suggest or imply a notion of the self as an integrated entity. A more "decentralized" conception of the self, for example, can help sensitize us to the multiple ways in which the "same" individual perceives and responds to a loss, in sometimes conflicting or ambivalent fashion.

At the level of the family, grieving is a public as well as private act, one whose expression is regulated by norms of family interaction, family roles, hierarchies of power, support and other features of family structure and process (cf., Walsh and McGoldrick, 1991). Even such apparently "private" experiences as remembering the deceased have a collective dimension, as stories told about the family member who has died become part of the public record of that person's life, shaping as well as codifying memories and their possible disputation by various family members.

Personal and family responses to loss can be best understood against the backdrop of broader community and cultural interpretations of death and loss, the expectations imposed on bereaved persons, and the norms that regulate the mourning process. At times the influence of the broader society on the grief experience is subtle and abstract, as in implicit expectations for how someone of a particular gender, age or ethnicity will grieve (Stroebe, 1992), while at other times, appropriate grief behavior is systematically delineated (e.g., Wolowelsky, 1996). Such cultural and community constructions of particular losses may also be contradictory, as when societal beliefs recognize the special poignancy of the accidental death of a child, but the local media implicitly blame the parents for allowing it to happen.

Clara's and Kerry's experiences illustrate the interactions of various levels of these systems. The concept of self as a multifaceted entity is most evident in the case of Kerry, who came to sharply delineate a more extroverted self seen by the world, and a more introverted self experienced in quiet moments of reflection. Much of the transformation experienced across the course of her son's chronic illness and through the bereavement that followed had to do with tapping the resources of this deeper but quieter voice within her. The impact of family roles, on the other hand, is more striking in the case of Clara, whose long-standing role as the one who gave selflessly to others contributed to painful complications in her relationship to her failing husband. Ed's angry demands in the nursing home, while no longer backed by the threat of physical assault, were consistent with his well-established position of power and domination in the family. Clara's son Richard also played an important role in her struggle, pushing insistently for her to "cut herself off" from a man who had chronically abused her. Kerry's family relationships, on the other hand, were conspicuously absent from her account of her grieving, raising questions about who in her life served to validate her view of the meaning of her loss or supported her in her quest for a deeper and wiser sense of herself. Ultimately, for both Clara and Kerry, these personal and family factors were nested within broader societal constructions of the appropriate role of women as caretakers, although the restrictions of this role were more keenly felt by Clara, as a function of both ethnic expectations and gender stereotyping.

In summary, the reconstruction of a personal world of meaning in the wake of loss must take into account ongoing relationships with real and symbolic others, as well as the resources of the mourners themselves. We are faced with the task of transforming our identities so as to redefine our symbolic connection to the deceased while maintaining our relationship with the living (Klass et al., 1996). Our attempts to do so may resonate or be dissonant with the views of others, such as immediate family or more distant social contacts. To understand even the most private dimensions of loss, we must place them in a social context that supports, opposes, or ignores our experience and need to change. Conflicts in these social contexts contribute to difficulties in adapting to loss, whereas consonance in the multiple social circles affected by the loss can support a more coherent revision of our life narratives.

Conclusion

In this brief chapter I have tried to introduce the outlines of an emerging perspective on grief, one that stands in some contrast to traditional theories that focus on general stages, tasks or symptoms that are presumed to have relevance to all bereaved persons. Instead, I have tried to place inflection on the extent to which adaptation to loss is shaped by personal, familial and cultural factors that are too often marginalized in efforts to formalize and standardize our models. In taking this stance, I have suggested that meaning reconstruction is the central process of grieving, and have offered a few preliminary principles for the construction of a more adequate theory compatible with this perspective. Finally, I have tried to illustrate some of the propositions that derive from such a constructivist account of loss by drawing upon the experience of two women who have faced chronic loss in two of its many forms. But ultimately, this effort is only part of a larger reorientation in grief theory that is underway on the part of clinicians, theorists, and researchers, one that will take some years to coalesce into a more satisfying model. I hope that this chapter contributes to this trend, and that in its own way it will help advance a richer and more idiographic understanding of loss and its role in human life.

Healing Rituals: Pathways to Wholeness During Prolonged Illness and Following Death

13

The Reverend Alice Parsons Zulli, C.T. and
O. Duane Weeks, Ph.D.

*A llison and her husband, Kenneth, were nearing the comple-
tion of a nightmare journey through the bizarre, labyrin-
thine experience of brain cancer. Ken was only 32 years old, a
promising young attorney and a physical fitness buff. Allison was
a kindergarten teacher. Their lives had been cruelly interrupted
when Ken suffered a seizure at the gym. Myriad tests and agonizing hours spent waiting for results ended with the diagnosis of
an inoperable brain tumor. Six short months and three hospital
stays later, Ken asked Allison to let him die at home.*

*The seizures were controlled by medications, but Ken's
memory had deteriorated and he became progressively agitated.
Allison discovered that by massaging Ken's body with warm oil
while playing their favorite music, rather than administering
sedation, Ken became less restless and seemed to arrive at a place
of total peace during these ministrations. Thus, a ritual was born.*

*Five or six times each day, Allison was able to show her deep
love for Ken by calming his tortured body with massage and
music. Six weeks after Allison discovered the effectiveness of their
massage ritual, Ken died. As she massaged his legs for the last*

time, with tears streaming down her face, she received tremendous satisfaction, fulfillment, even joy at being able to help Ken leave this world with great dignity, comfort, and love.

All people suffer loss, and most suffer a loss through death, which may come sooner or later, suddenly or expectedly, privately or publicly. Death is as much a part of life as birth, and therefore the experience of a death loss becomes one of the defining moments of our lives. Recovery, or healing, from a loss by death does not mean that we resume the way we lived and felt prior to the loss. Rather, true healing comes through discovering how it is possible to live with, and be enlarged by, the loss.

Healing is finding wholeness. Those who have experienced a death often feel as if something is missing from their lives; a part has been taken from the whole. Their lives may feel shattered. Healing is the process of reorganizing lives into a form of wholeness by incorporating, but not fixating on, the loss.

Rituals are threads that weave together the fabric of a society. A ritual may be viewed as a "container" that can hold the grief experience while the loss is integrated with the changes it has caused. In our society, ceremonies and rituals generally mark the passage of time, special events, or significant changes in status or profession, or they may reflect our traditions and beliefs. As an outward and visible sign of a change in life or an affirmation of belief, ceremonies symbolically connect us to our traditions and our community.

The word *ritual* comes from the Sanskrit *rita*, which refers to both art and order. Like all real art, ritual provides organic order, a pattern of dynamic expression (Houston, 1987).

Nearly all of us belong to families and communities. We attend schools and work in businesses. We worship in churches, mosques, or synagogues. We join others at concerts, ball games, or classes. We make acquaintances and become friends. We date, love, and marry, and belong to new families in new communities, attending new schools and working in new places. We are, in short, social beings with a great deal of dependence on one another. Perhaps John Donne said it best when he wrote that "No man is an island entire of itself;

every man is a piece of the continent, a part of the main . . ." (Donne, Meditation XVII). Because we are not independent islands, we need more than biological chance or happenstance to determine our relationships. We need rituals to provide us with ties to others. By tying us to others, rituals can help us determine who we are, from where we came, and where we may be going.

> The rituals in our lives contribute to our changing sense of ourselves over time, while also connecting us to the generations who came before us. They are a bridge capable of linking our history, our present lives, and what we most hope for our children, our grandchildren, and our great-grandchildren (Imber-Black and Roberts, 1992, p. 305–6).

Whenever something is lost or destroyed, ritual can not only provide a means of processing grief in its many forms, but can also be a supportive structure to bring comfort and healing. When the loss is a death loss, it involves the physical, emotional, social, and spiritual dimensions of life. Special death rituals can be incorporated to assist in the healing process after a loss of this magnitude.

How Death Rituals Help

Death rituals serve slightly different purposes than those described above by Imber-Black and Roberts. Death rituals do bind us together with other mourners in our common grief, but they can also facilitate separation from the person who has died. Like graduation or wedding ceremonies, many death rituals are, at the same time, rituals of binding and release.

When we experience the death of someone close to us, we are no longer whole; there is a rent in the fabric of our lives. The feelings generated by this loss cannot easily be relieved without the help of death rituals. Death rituals serve to ". . . catalyze acute grief responses, prescribe structural behaviors in time of flux, and encourage recognition of the loss and development of new relationships with both the deceased and the community" (Rando, 1984, p. 190). A community can provide social support and validate the grief of family mourners when someone has died, such as the expressions of social support following the Oklahoma City bombing. Death and loss must be validated in order for healing to occur.

Additionally, death rituals are a means " . . . to separate the living from the dead, (and) to provide the survivors with impetus to continue their lives . . ." (Sanders, 1989, p. 96). As Imber-Black and Roberts (1992) argue that rituals in general are ". . . capable of linking our history, our present lives, and what we most hope for . . .," the same may be said for death rituals (p. 305). Those who participate in these death rituals will derive a sense of intergenerational progression, with an appreciation for the past, a responsibility for the present, and a commitment to the future.

When we think of death rituals, we usually think of a funeral or memorial service that occurs soon after death. There are, however, rituals that take place prior to a death that can facilitate the progression towards healing.

How Pre-Death Rituals Help

While post-death rituals only benefit survivors, most pre-death ceremonies have the major advantage of being participated in and valued by both the dying person and the survivors. This advantage is especially important to the dying and those significant people in their lives, who are living through the experience of long-term illness and anticipating the finality of death.

When a loved one is dying there will be sadness, and the response to that sadness may depend largely on previous experiences with death. When something produces anxiety, such as receiving a diagnosis of cancer and a prognosis of death, there may be the temptation to distort or ignore the information in an attempt to use denial as a coping mechanism. Perhaps friends and family members try to provide comfort with platitudes of "being strong," "getting through," or "not leaving them." While well meaning, these cliches only serve to isolate the dying person from the nurturing and care so desperately sought. Physical changes cause many emotional difficulties for the dying person, as well as for family and friends.

The dying person may have specific needs or wishes that should be addressed in order for him or her to live as wholly as possible and die with a sense that life's course has been completed. Upon realizing these needs or wishes, the dying person may communicate them with a sense of urgency. If communication is clear, the needs are usually met. However, if the dying person is under medical care, and his or her anxiety, agitation or dying process becomes too upsetting, a familiar response is to sedate the patient, and sometimes members of the family as well. Sedation can temporarily relieve anxiety and agitation, but it is only a stop-gap measure, and may well inhibit the ability to understand the issues that need reconciliation and closure.

One way to discover the dying person's needs is to encourage memory work and life review. It may be helpful for someone close to the dying person to listen to the pain and explore the feelings about this unwanted journey into death. An oral or mental inventory of life's accomplishments and disappointments may help the dying person understand unresolved feelings. Such an inventory provides a wonderful basis for a life history that can be treasured and saved for future generations. Through this process, the caregiver may find an incentive to do some personal life review.

> Most people, as they're dying, want to feel that their having been alive has been significant, that they made some difference in this world and in the lives of those around them and for us, some periodic review of how our lives are going, and recognition of our achievements, may help us find more enjoyment and purpose in our lives. At the same time some recognition of our 'unfinished business' or troubled relationships may lead us to try to heal some problem areas now, rather than waiting until we are dying. This could enrich our lives and prevent frantic attempts at reconciliation when it is almost too late (Callanan and Kelley, 1992, p. 153).

Caregivers may encounter feelings of helplessness, anger or resentment toward others whose lives seem untouched by illness. Dying people may be trying to complete unfinished business or reconciliation, or they may need to feel secure about their family's preparedness. In order to resolve these feelings, the dying need a sense of control and should be given as many choices as possible. Pre-death ritual can provide the dying with an avenue to a peaceful and loving death.

In a soft but firm voice, the frail old woman spoke of her love for her Lord, and the importance of her religious beliefs. Then sitting quietly in her chair, she listened carefully as her children and grandchildren told her what she meant to them and how much they loved her. As each recalled a fond memory or related a special story, she often wiped tears from her eyes and occasionally smiled gently. Her family expressed their sorrow that they would have to let her go. There was, as a pastor expressed later, "a great deal of love evident" during that ritual.

The frail old woman was a Lutheran, and she, her family and her pastor were participating in a pre-death ritual called Communion for the Dying. After stories and expressions of love were shared around the circle, family members joined together, for one final time, in a communion service involving all of them. The following morning, the old woman was asked what she thought of the ritual. "Oh," she replied, "I thought about it this morning, and the thinking was almost as good as the actual doing." One of her grandsons related that, because of his concern for his grandmother, he had been having trouble sleeping. The night after the communion ritual, he slept soundly throughout the night. This ritual, then, provided several benefits. The dying woman derived a great deal of pride and satisfaction from the love expressed by her family members. She was able to share her faith in a way that was meaningful to her and to the others, and to experience the love expressed through the ceremony. This pre-death ritual also helped her family members acknowledge the eminent death of the woman.

Religious entities often incorporate rituals that have been developed over long periods of time. Once the rituals have been incorporated into religious traditions, they are used by followers of that tradition. The dying are often lonely and depressed, beset by nameless fears, and, like the woman in the illustration above, they welcome the light and hope brought by their spiritual caregiver. Kindness, gentleness, and empathy are important, as is the reassurance that the caregiver really cares, and God cares even more.

The dying person needs particular consideration. As societal taboos about death begin to be broken down, we are able to embrace the dying and their families as they face oncoming death openly.

The dying person should be able to set the tone for the visit. He or she may want to talk about death or release a burden. This may be a time when the ritual of confession is heard, or there may be a ritual of prayers for strength, rest, awareness of God's presence, or for peace of mind and spirit. This may also be time for a significant commitment ritual, like the ritual of Holy Baptism.

As beings with limitless creative potential, we mark transitions and change of seasons with cherished rituals. These rituals can implement pathways for real and symbolic ways to express feelings. Can we not use these rituals to address the emotional, mental, and spiritual quest of the person facing death, as well as the survivors?

Some pre-death rituals, like prayer, can be practiced alone. Others, like the Communion for the Dying, involve several people. Some are planned, others are relatively spontaneous. Some have religious connotations, others are secular, and they may also benefit different people at different times.

Jim was an avid fisherman all of his life and active in his church community. When he learned that he was dying from a lung disease, he carefully and thoughtfully sorted through all his fishing tackle, separating it into one dozen different tackle boxes. He then donated the tackle boxes to his church for their annual spring auction. Jim died the week before the auction, but his fishing tackle brought high prices from Jim's church friends who bid on them as a memorial to Jim.

Jim's self-made ritual of arranging and distributing his beloved fishing tackle benefited him, the recipients of the tackle boxes, and the church coffers. Had he not thought of preparing his tackle for the auction, it would probably have been forgotten or discarded, and neither Jim nor his friends at church would have received the emotional and other benefits that this pre-death ritual provided.

Some suggestions for pre-death rituals:

1. **Journaling.** In the novel *The Bridges of Madison County,* the heroine journaled her feelings for years, including the recall of a brief but meaningful interlude with a stranger. After her death, these journals served as a vehicle for teaching her children who their

mother really was and what she wanted done with her cremated remains.

2. **Meditation.** As a vehicle for strengthening the immune system and developing inner peace, meditation may be an extremely helpful ritual for those with catastrophic and long-term illnesses, illnesses that are tremendously detrimental to a sense of health and well-being.

3. **Photographs and videos.** Looking through pictures offers a chance for memory work and life review.

4. **Possessions inventory.** This provides an opportunity to indicate where personal possessions should go and, perhaps, an opportunity to bestow them on the recipients prior to death.

5. **Journeys.** The opportunity to see, or do something important, perhaps for the last time, can be a meaningful experience.

6. **Sacraments of communion, anointing, baptism.** These spiritually fundamental rituals, as those of other faiths and traditions, can provide needed for comfort, closure and peace for the dying person or the survivors.

We can even design rituals that clearly mark passings or losses. One father, in a small ceremony, actually turned his checkbook over to his daughter, signifying that he gave her control over his finances.

How Post-Death Rituals Help

As important as pre-death rituals are to the dying and those in a significant relationship with them, post-death rituals are just as important to a wide range of survivors.

Funerals are the most well-known post-death rituals. In death, the pain of loss will not be denied, and the funeral begins the lengthy process of integrating the bereaved back into the community. The funeral offers a tribute to the deceased, emphasizing the worth of that person; it allows the community to provide social support; and it affirms social order in that, while a death has occurred, the community continues to function.

There is much more involved when putting closure to an individual's life than a funeral or memorial service. The creation and implementation of personal ceremony can add another dimension to the healing journey through grief. These ceremonies speak to the subconscious mind in a symbolic manner, much like a dream, since "[T]he subconscious does not distinguish between what is real and what is vividly imagined" (Paladin, 1991, p. 56). By acting out the change on a physical level (ritual), the mind knows what is wanted. Whenever a ritual is created to restore life's balance, it is important to verbalize the contents of that ritual, because putting changes into words impresses the mind. Furthermore, whenever others are invited to witness the rituals or ceremonies, the seriousness of one's intentions is communicated to the mind.

Paladin (1991) discusses the importance of ritual as a means of letting go and moving on, an important goal of death rituals:

> We're physical beings. It is natural for us to express ourselves with physical actions. The mind and body are one. When we feel helpless about an event that's happened, we suffer. We experience "disease" because we have lost our sense of control, our balance of emotional and physical energy . . . Whenever we experience a transition, happy or sad, a ceremony helps us recenter ourselves by making a symbolic statement about that change. By doing so we understand that it is time to let go of the old and move on to the new (p. 6).

Many years ago it was customary for the dead body to be "laid out" in the family parlor for a few days prior to burial. In the past four or five decades, however, this ritual has fallen into disfavor, due in part to this culture's aversion to death and society's delegation of death work to funeral directors and cemetery workers, as well as stringent laws and regulations.

Charla was a lovely 26-year-old woman with Down's Syndrome. She had lived with her parents all her life, and they lovingly cared for her during her long illness and subsequent death. Because Charla's parents and siblings wanted to experience the death rituals more personally, they chose to have Charla's body returned to their home for a three-day visitation prior to her funeral.

Charla's mother, father and sister carefully dressed her, combed her hair, and, along with her brother, tenderly placed her body in the casket. Charla's body was then returned to the bedroom of her family home, where friends and family called for the next three days. During those days, many friends came by to see Charla and visit the family in their home, sharing memories of their young friend. The night before Charla's funeral service, her parents took their pillows and blanket into Charla's room, where they spent their last night with her, sleeping beside her casket.

By returning to the practice of holding the visitation ritual in their home, Charla's parents, along with her siblings, were able to receive the benefits of receiving visitors in the comfort of their own home, while feeling the great satisfaction of having Charla's body in her own room, with them, during the last few days they would all spend together. Participation in this ritual has continued to provide a great deal of solace to Charla's parents.

Susie's story is another example of how a healing ritual can help move survivors toward wholeness. A bereaved daughter, Susie worked with her grief counselor to develop a healing ritual.

Susie was grieving her mother's death from breast cancer. Even though she had lived with her mother during her illness, spent quality time with her mother, and she and her siblings had gathered around her mother at the time of death, loving, talking, praying and crying, one obstacle remained in Susie's way. She could not bring herself to return to the quaint seaside village where she and her mother had ritually gone twice every year. With strong support and suggestions from her trusted grief counselor, Susie mustered her courage and retraced the drive to the resort, including stopping at their favorite restaurant for lunch. Although she was unable to eat much, she felt encouraged that she could go in, sit down and stay for awhile. She spent time browsing through their favorite shops and, unexpectedly, found herself sharing her purpose for being there with a gentle-voiced shopkeeper. Susie searched for and found the perfect card and a tiny gift that she knew her mother would have loved, said good-bye to the shopkeeper, and drove to the beach. She found a quiet, secluded stretch of sand and tearfully wrote her feelings for her mother on the card, enclosed the tiny gift, sealed the envelope, and buried it deeply in the sand. As her tears dried, Susie experienced a sense of peace and joy that she had not felt in a long time.

That was over a year ago; Susie has enjoyed short visits to that seaside village many times and continues to remember her mother with joy and gladness rather than paralyzing sadness.

Some Suggestions for Post-Death Rituals

1. **Wake/Celebration of life/Visitation.** This ritual varies according to ethnic and cultural expectations. It allows friends and family members to rejoice in the fact that the deceased person lived.
2. **Funeral/Memorial service.** These rituals provide social support for the mourners and the opportunity for members of the community to express love and regret. They are very important, both in a social and individual sense.
3. **Funeral/Burial tasks.** Within the funeral ceremony, there are significant rituals in which mourners or close friends can participate. Reading, singing, carrying the casket, folding a veteran's flag, placing dirt on the coffin, dedicating the grave—all are helpful rituals.
4. **Taking food to the surviving family.** This is a ritual of kindness and support for the bereaved family and customary in this country. However, some spiritual belief systems do not view bringing food as an acceptable practice.
5. **Flowers and donations.** These contributions are commonly accepted at the funeral, or shortly before or after, and show tender concern and care for the family.
6. **Anniversaries of remembrance.** Rituals on special occasions, such as holidays, the anniversary of the death, the deceased's birthday or wedding anniversary, graduations, weddings, and births of the deceased's children; all support surviving family members and friends by emphasizing the importance of the one who has died.

Who Needs Ritual?

There is a common belief that a ritual must either be a formal ceremony or one that is strange and unfamiliar, and some may hesitate to embrace the idea that rituals may be helpful to them. What they may overlook is their participation in rituals that have become ordinary markers in their day-to-day lives, such as birthday, anniversary, or graduation celebrations. And while some may fear the exploration of rituals, there is greater reason to learn how they may be helpful. For example, a dying person will often try to protect the survivors by requesting that no services be held after the death. On the contrary, it is often necessary for survivors of a death to participate in some type of ritual to remember the person who has died and to assist them along a healing journey.

Rituals can be especially important to those who may be grieving but do not have traditional relationships or ways to express their grief. Disenfranchised grief is a manifestation of society's belief that, in order to receive permission to grieve a loss, the loss needs to be appropriate by societal dictates. Thus, "disenfranchisement can occur when a society inhibits grief by establishing 'grieving norms' that deny such emotions to persons deemed to have insignificant losses, insignificant relationships, or an insignificant capacity to grieve" (Doka, 1989, xv).

Disenfranchisement can occur through divorce, break-up, pet loss, loss of a lover, ex-spouse, colleague, co-worker, friend, or death of a non-biological child or parent. "In more complex societies, funeral rituals are no longer communal but familial, and as a result the right to express grief is limited to those in recognized kin roles. The grief of others is disenfranchised" (Doka, 1989, xv).

How to Develop a Death Ritual

Why have rituals, in one form or another, been practiced for many thousands of years? How do rituals fulfill the deep needs of the terminally ill and their survivors? What are those needs?

There are six basic categories, or dimensions, of death needs: spiritual, psychological, social, ethnic/cultural, physical, and financial.

For example, a young man is dying of cancer. He desires (needs) to be hugged. That need is physical. The yearning for human touch is also psychological, as it fulfills a need to be nurtured. It is also social, as it requires more than just oneself to interact. Depending on the beliefs of the young man and those with whom he is interacting, his need to be hugged can also be cultural and spiritual.

Rituals have also been categorized by Imber-Black and Roberts (1992) according to five purposes: relating, changing, healing, believing, and celebrating. These categories, like the needs listed above, are not exclusive, and a death ritual might be a ritual of relating (to other mourners), changing (death changes relationships), healing (leading toward wholeness), believing (spiritual affirmation), and celebrating (the life that has been lived).

". . . [R]ituals have the capacity to hold and express contradictions" (Imber-Black and Roberts, 1992, p. 303). You can use a ritual to reflect on the past and, forgetting or limiting the influence of the past, move more fully into the present.

How to Create a Ritual

1. **Focus on a goal.** The first step is to get a clear sense of what you want to do and what outcome you desire. What would you like to experience? Your goal should be simple and realistic; if it is complicated, work toward the outcome in stages. Repetition empowers a ritual.

2. **Plan.** Think about what is needed and how it may be achieved in order to know yourself better and discover what is important to you. Decide whether or not you want others to participate, how much time will be involved, where this ritual will take place and, if using symbols, which ones will best represent your needs.

3. **Prepare.** By going through the physical, mental, and emotional aspects of preparing your plan, you are fine-tuning your plan. Physically, you must find symbols and the setting; mentally, you must refine the details; and emotionally, you must confront the emotions that will arise from this process. Your ritual will allow you to access, express, and transform the most difficult feelings

in a way that comforts both you and those who participate on your behalf.

4. **Manifest.** When the manifestation of a ritual includes using, making, or receiving something tangible, it becomes easier to shift into the end-process of incorporation. The tangible object will still be important and offer a sense of connection, even when the ceremony has been completed.

5. **Evaluate.** Take time to process the effects of your ritual. Are you noticing a shift in feeling, thinking, or acting? Are your feelings more manageable? Have your daily habits normalized? If so, your ritual may be helping.

6. **Incorporate.** C. S. Lewis tells the following story that illustrates incorporation as an ongoing process.

> . . . a burly, cheerful labouring man, carrying a hoe and a watering pot came into our churchyard, and, as he pulled the gate behind him, shouted over his shoulder to two friends, "See you later, I'm just going to visit Mum." He meant he was going to weed and water and generally tidy up her grave . . . A six-by-three foot flower-bed had become Mum. That was his symbol for her, his link with her. Caring for it was visiting her (Lewis, 1943).

This man had originally planted flowers on his mother's grave as part of a ceremony to let him honor his mother as he said good-bye to her. As time passed, he felt his relationship with his mother was not over, and he needed to keep the love and connection they'd had when she was alive. Visiting a cemetery makes death very real, and his visits would take on the form of a gradual separation and transition to being motherless in his real world.

A Final Thought on the Importance of Death Rituals

Imber-Black and Roberts, discussing rituals in general, touch on the importance of death rituals as a means of finding our place in history and the social order, as well as helping us retain our individual identities.

The rituals in our lives contribute to our changing sense of ourselves over time, while also connecting us to the generations who came before us. . . . You may want to think about your family and your culture's ritual life a hundred years from now, a time when human beings will still be making rituals. As perhaps no other aspect of life can do, it is our rituals that simultaneously connect us with what is universal in human experience, while allowing our own unique personhood, family, ethnic group, and culture to emerge (Imber-Black and Roberts, 1992, p. 305–306).

Doug Manning has written that, "those who avoid funeral rituals have their funerals on their psychiatrist's couch" (Manning, 1995, p.4). The lack of participation in funerals or other death rituals may result in a separation from the community of mourners and an inability to grieve constructively. Therefore, in reality, the effort of avoiding death rites becomes a harmful, rather than a helpful, exercise.

Alternatively, death rituals can be the springboard to a renewed sense of the richness of life.

Elinor was a beautiful woman, a gifted artist, and devoted wife. After thirty years of marriage to David, Elinor was diagnosed with colon cancer on May 1st and, by December 3rd, had undergone surgery followed by chemotherapy, gently said her goodbyes, and died. David was devastated. He vacuumed the carpets frequently because he could scream and cry and the neighbors remained unaware of his pain. With great trepidation he joined a support group and learned that grieving is a process and, at the appropriate time, rituals of closure can be helpful in moving away from the death.

For months, David struggled to find balance and became a remarkable, although somewhat obsessive, housekeeper, with the exception of one obstacle. Elinor's favorite shoes remained in place by her side of the bed, and he could not bring himself to throw them away. Every day they were a reminder of the incredible emptiness in David's life.

Many months later, David stared at the shoes and knew what he needed to do. He found a small box to put them in, added a pair of his own shoes, and climbed the hill behind his house where he and Elinor had buried their beloved cats, Freddie, Squirt, and Ziz, creating a sacred place of memories. There David dug a hole and, through his tears, placed the shoes in the hole and said good-bye to Elinor and the life that used to be.

Two weeks later, David shared his story in the support group and let them know he was ready to move into life.

Both the dying and those with significant relationships to them, as well as bereaved survivors, who participate in death rituals are likely to gain considerable psychological and emotional comfort from such involvements. They will experience increased social ties, a personal sense of belonging, and validation and support of their own grief work.

What we call the beginning is often the end. And to make an end is to make a beginning. End is where we start. . .
—Eliot

Conclusion

There are very few of us whose lives will not be touched by prolonged, life-threatening illness. The chapters in this book touch
on a variety of issues we can expect to face: the process of "fading
away"; the implications of traumatic stress and cognitive processing
in anticipatory grief; the need to make informed and ethical decisions in a time of confusion and powerlessness; the importance of
sensitizing ourselves to cultural differences of patients and their families; the complex and painful ramifications of such illnesses as HIV/
AIDS, Alzheimer's, and cancer; the particular needs of children and
adolescents in times of loss; the search for meaning in the face of
grief; and pathways to hope and healing of the spirit.

While dealing with the myriad aspects of dying, death and bereavement, these articles have in common the imperative for us to
begin to view ourselves and our world in a different way. Whether
referring to "meaning reconstruction," the "redefinition of self," or
the "stimulation of necessary internal and external change," they all
call upon us to reenvision how we live, heal and die.

Author Joan Borysenko expressed it eloquently by saying, "We
in the health care and caregiving communities frequently encounter
people with life-threatening illnesses at the point when they are no
longer who they have been and are not yet reborn into who they will
be. We meet them in the space between 'no longer' and 'not yet.'"
She suggests that in this alien and frightening territory both the patient and their loved ones are extremely suggestible and search for
clues everywhere—in everything we do and say and how we do and
say it. That creates the potential for us to do either great good or

great harm, so it is of utmost importance to be both sensitive and mindful in our interaction with them (Borysenko, 1996).

A terminal illness or the loss of a loved one shakes us to our core and compels us to ask questions that seem to have no answers. Victor Frankl has said that crisis without meaning equals despair; but even when there is no longer hope for a cure, there is still the possibility of deep healing of the spirit and the opportunity to engage in growth both during and after the illness.

Miss Mildred's story reminds us that we must enter the dying person's world cautiously and with respect, keeping open to issues and alternatives that we have perhaps not considered or will need to consider from a different viewpoint. In the process, we learn the valuable lesson that, as Price offers, "tolerance is a robust and demanding virtue." How, then, do we navigate in these deep and often turbulent waters? A wise and learned teacher once told me that it is most valuable to regard one's knowledge base not as a means of possessing the answers, but as a springboard for formulating thoughtful questions. That is an empowering concept—something we can all do, whatever our backgrounds.

These authors remind us that this is a gratifying and exciting time to be involved in the field of thanatology. There is heightened awareness of how important it is to validate, both publicly and privately, the experiences and multiple losses of dying and death, enabling us to embrace the dying and their loved ones as they face death more openly. Hearteningly, several of the contributors have noted the increasing recognition of ritual as a powerful tool in dealing with grief and mourning.

It is an honor to accompany others on this difficult journey and to share in their learning new coping strategies and finding their own ways to face profound loss. As Price so movingly expresses, "[People] are often . . . inspiring in their bravery and selfless devotion . . . Despite the fact that nothing in their short lives has prepared them for this . . . they master their urge to flee and face into an ordeal that one might expect would overwhelm them . . . To work with such people . . . is a great and humbling privilege."

To translate the "difficult lessons of agony from our head to our heart," as Rando tells us, is "part of the transformative power of grief and mourning." We observe how Kerry, a young mother, experiences a transformation during her son's terminal illness. What a gift it is when the potential for profound growth and transformation informs our understanding of the process of coming to terms with death and saying goodbye. The Pulitzer Prize-winning poet Mary Oliver (1992) has written, "This is our failure, that in all the world/ Only the stricken have learned how to grieve."

Resource List

AIDS Information Network
1211 Chestnut Street, 7th Floor, Philadelphia, PA 19107
(215) 575-1110, Library extension 131
E-mail: aidsinfo@critpath.org
AIDS Information Network has projects related to education and prevention of HIV/AIDS and maintains a comprehensive multi-media, multi-lingual collection of over 100,000 items related to HIV/AIDS. Information requests are answered by professional staff on site, or via telephone, fax, mail or e-mail.

ALS Association National Office
21021 Ventura Blvd., Suite 321, Woodland Hills, CA 91364
(818) 340-7500
http://www.alsa.org
The Amyotrophic Lateral Sclerosis (ALS) Association is dedicated to the fight against ALS, commonly referred to as Lou Gehrig's disease. The Association is a national information resource on ALS, funding research and providing referrals for counseling, training and support.

Alzheimer's Association
919 N. Michigan Avenue, Suite 1000, Chicago, IL 60611-1676
(800) 272-3900
The Alzheimer's Association is the only national voluntary organization dedicated to conquering Alzheimer's disease through research, and through providing education and support to people

with Alzheimer's disease, their families and caregivers. The Association sends out general information about the disease and caregiving responsibilities and refers callers to their local chapter where they can get support group information and find out about resources in their area.

American Brain Tumor Association

2720 River Road, Suite 146, Des Plaines, IL 60018
(800) 886-2282
http://pubweb.acns.nwu.edu/~lberko/abta_html/abta1.htm
The American Brain Tumor Association is a not-for-profit organization offering over 20 publications which address brain tumors, their treatment, and coping with the disease; nationwide listing of support groups and physicians offering investigative treatments; regional Town Hall meetings; and a pen-pal program.

American Cancer Society

1599 Clifton Road, NE, Atlanta, GA 30329-4251
(800) ACS-2345
http://www.cancer.org
The American Cancer Society is the nationwide, community-based voluntary health organization dedicated to eliminating cancer as a major health problem by preventing cancer, saving lives and diminishing suffering from cancer through research, education, advocacy, and service.

American Heart Association

7272 Greenville Avenue, Dallas, TX 75231
(214) 373-6300 or (800)AHA-USA1 to be connected to closest affiliate in area
http://www.americanheart.org
The American Heart Association is one of the world's premier health organizations committed to reducing disability and death from cardiovascular diseases and stroke.

American Liver Foundation

1425 Pompton Avenue, Cedar Grove, NJ 07009
(800) 223-0179
http://www.liverfoundation.org
A national non-profit organization dedicated to preventing,
treating, and curing hepatitis and other liver and gallbladder
diseases through research and education.

American Lung Association

1740 Broadway, New York, NY 10019-4374
(212) 315-8700
http://www.lungusa.org
E-mail: info@lungusa.org
The mission of the American Lung Association is to prevent lung
disease and promote lung health with a nationwide highest priority
on asthma. The American Lung Association has been fighting lung
disease for more than 90 years, providing programs of education,
community service, advocacy and research.

American Parkinson Disease Association, Inc.

1250 Hylan Blvd., Suite 4B, Staten Island, NY 10305-1946
(718) 981-8001 or (800)223-2732
E-mail: apda@admin.con2.com
APDA is a not-for-profit voluntary health agency committed to
serving the Parkinson community through a comprehensive
program of research, education and support, offering educational
booklets and supplements, symposiums, and referrals to support
groups, local chapters, and physicians specializing in Parkinson's
disease throughout the United States.

Association for Death Education and Counseling

638 Prospect Ave., Hartford, CT 06105
(860) 586-7503
http://www.adec.org
ADEC is dedicated to improving the quality of death education
and death related counseling and caregiving; to promoting the
development and interchange of related theory and research; and

to providing support, stimulation and encouragement to its members and those studying and working in the death related fields.

Bereavement and Hospice Support Netline

http://www.ubalt.edu/www/bereavement
The Bereavement and Hospice Support Netline is a web page listing of bereavement support groups and services listed by state within eleven different bereavement group types. Only no-fee bereavement support groups and no-fee or nominal fee bereavement services and newsletters will be listed. There is an Add-A-Resource Form and a Correction and Comment Form in the web page if you have any suggestions or want to add a support service in your area to the list.

Candlelighters Childhood Cancer Foundation

7910 Woodmont Ave., Suite 460, Bethesda, MD 20814-3015
(800) 366-2223 or (301) 657-8401
http://www.candlelighters.org
CCCF provides support, information, and advocacy to families of children with cancer (at any stage of the illness or who are bereaved), to professionals in the field, and to adult survivors, through local groups, newsletters, and other services.

Children's Hospice International

2202 Mt. Vernon Ave., Suite 3C, Alexandria, VA 22301
(703) 684-0330
http://www.chionline.org
E-Mail: chiorg@aol.com
Children's Hospice International creates a world of hospice support for children, providing medical and technical assistance, research, and education for these special children, their families and health care professionals. CHI works with hospices, children's hospitals, homecare agencies and other individuals and organizations to assist them in better caring for children with life threatening conditions.

The Compassionate Friends, Inc.

P.O. Box 3696, Oak Brook, IL 60522-3696

(630) 990-0010

http://pages.prodigy.com/CA/lycq97a/lycq97tcf.html

The Compassionate Friends is a self-help organization whose purpose is to offer friendship and understanding to parents and siblings following the death of a child. They have 580 chapters nationwide which provide monthly meetings, phone contacts, lending libraries and a local newsletter. The national organization provides newsletters, distributes grief-related materials, and answers requests for referrals and information.

Cystic Fibrosis Foundation

6931 Arlington Road, Bethesda, MD 20814

(800) 344-4823

The mission of the Cystic Fibrosis Foundation (CFF) is to assure the development of the means to cure and control cystic fibrosis and to improve the quality of life for those with the disease.

The Dougy Center

P.O. Box 86582, Portland, OR 97286

(503) 775-5683

E-mail: help@dougy.org

The Dougy Center provides support groups for grieving children that are age specific (3-5, 6-12, teens) and loss specific (parent death, sibling death, survivors of homicide/violent death, survivors of suicide). They have additional services that include national trainings, consultations to schools and organizations, crisis-line information, and referrals.

Gay Men's Health Crisis

129 W. 20th Street, New York, NY 10011

(212) 807-6664

Gay Men's Health Crisis is the nation's oldest and largest AIDS service organization and is a model for AIDS care, education, and advocacy world wide. GMHC offers a multitude of support services, including legal assistance, nutritional counseling, family services and crisis intervention. GMHC sponsors a AIDS Hot Line number, (212) 807-6655. Operators provide free one-on-one counseling, answer questions, provide referrals and guidance.

Gilda's Club

195 W. Houston Street, New York, NY 10014
(212) 647-9700
E-mail: mannheim@walrus.com
Gilda's Club is a psychosocial support community for people with cancer, their families and friends, offering support, meditation and networking groups, pot-luck suppers, and social events. Everything is entirely free. There are special programs for children whose parents or family members have cancer or who have cancer themselves. They have ten affiliates across the United States, Canada and London, and offer How-To-Start kits if anyone is interested in starting a Gilda's Club in their community.

Hospice Foundation of America

2001 S Street, NW, Suite 300, Washington, DC 20009
(202) 638-5419
http://www.hospicefoundation.org
The Hospice Foundation of America provides leadership in the development and application of hospice and its philosophy of care for terminally-ill people, conducting programs of education and providing grants for research projects. HFA sponsors an annual *Living With Grief* teleconference series, a monthly bereavement newsletter and other publications, and is in the process of developing a series of audio tapes on grief and bereavement for clergy.

In Loving Memory

1416 Green Run Lane, Reston, VA
(703) 435-0608
Mutual support, friendship and help for parents who have lost their only child or all of their children.

Leukemia Society of America
600 Third Ave., New York, NY 10016
(212) 573-8484
http://www.leukemia.org
Voluntary non-profit health organization to: cure leukemia and it's related cancers—lymphoma, multiple myeloma and Hodgkin's disease—and improve the quality of life of patients and their families.

Multiple Sclerosis Association of America
706 Haddonfield Rd, Cherry Hill, NJ 08002
(800) 833-4672
The Multiple Sclerosis Association of America is a national non-profit health care agency providing direct care services to those with MS. These services include a national toll-free hotline, peer counseling, support groups, therapeutic equipment loan program, educational literature, symptom management therapies and other vital services.

National Association of People with AIDS
1413 K Street, NW, Washington, DC 20036
(202)898-0414
http://www.thecure.org
NAPWA is a national AIDS advocacy group. They provide free publications on treatment and advocacy and have an extensive information and referral department that includes a fax-on-demand system; you can call (202)789-2222 from your fax machine to request information on HIV/AIDS. They also have a health and treatment department that provides up to date treatment information and a free bi-monthly publication, *Medical Alert* (available in English and Spanish.)

National Brain Tumor Foundation
785 Market St., Suite 1600, San Francisco, CA 94103
(800) 934-CURE or (415) 284-0208
The National Brain Tumor Foundation provides a variety of support and educational services for patients and their families,

including booklets, newsletters, support group listings and assistance starting new groups, a toll-free brain tumor information line, the Support Line patient/giver network, and national and regional conferences.

National Cancer Institute

9000 Rockville Pike, 31 Center Dr. - MSC 2580,
Bethesda, MD 20892-2580
(301) 496-5583 or (800) 422-6237
or TTY number (800) 332-8615
http://www.nci.nih.gov
The National Cancer Institute (NCI), the largest component of the National Institutes of Health, coordinates a national research program on cancer cause and prevention, detection and diagnosis, and treatment. In addition, NCI's mission includes dissemination of information about cancer to patients, the public, and health professionals, offering the Cancer Information Service (CIS). CIS meets the needs of patients, the public and health professionals through telephone service and an outreach program. Specially trained staff provide the latest scientific information in understandable language.

National Coalition for Cancer Survivorship

1010 Wayne Avenue, Suite 505, Silver Spring, MD 20910
(301) 650-8868
http://www.access.digex.net/~mkragen/cansearch.html
NCCS' mission is to improve the quality of life of people with all types of cancer. NCCS offers information on employment and insurance issues, provides referrals to sources of support and information, produces publications on survivorship issues, and advocates on behalf of cancer survivors before Congress and federal agencies.

National Hospice Organization
1901 N. Moore St., Suite 901, Arlington, VA 22209
(703) 243-5900
http://www.nho.org
NHO provides a broad range of services, including a referral
service to link individuals with hospices in their local communities, advocacy, and various educational publications and programs.

National Kidney Foundation
30 East 33rd St., New York, NY 10016
(800) 622-9010 or (212) 889-2210
http://www.kidney.org
The National Kidney Foundation seeks the means to the prevention of diseases of the kidney and urinary tract, while at the same
time ensuring that those now suffering from these diseases receive
the finest possible care. The Foundation supports research projects
and sponsors a wide variety of community programs in treatment,
service, education and prevention.

National Parkinson Foundation
1501 NW 9th Ave., Bob Hope Road, Miami, FL 33136
(800) 327-4545
http://www.parkinson.org
The National Parkinson Foundation's mission is fourfold: to find
the cause and cure for Parkinson's disease and other allied neurological disorders through research, to provide diagnostic and
therapeutic services, to improve the quality of life for patients
and caregivers, and to educate people about Parkinson's disease.

National Stroke Association
96 Inverness Dr. East, Suite 1, Englewood, CO 80112-5112
(303) 649-9299
http://www.stroke.org
National Stroke Association is the only national non-profit organization dedicating 100 percent of its resources to stroke, including
prevention, research, treatment and support for stroke survivors
and caregivers.

The International THEOS Foundation
(They Help Each Other Spiritually)
322 Blvd. Of the Allies, Suite 105, Pittsburgh, PA 15222
(412) 471-7779
THEOS helps persons whose spouses have died, providing educational materials and emotional support for the newly widowed.
Chapters offer ongoing self-help support groups. THEOS also
publishes a magazine series and hosts an annual national conference, open to both professionals and those who are recently
widowed.

Tragedy Assistance Program for Survivors, Inc.
2001 S Street, NW, Suite 300, Washington, DC 20009
(800) 959-TAPS
E-mail: TAPSHQ@aol.com
The Tragedy Assistance Program for Survivors, Inc. (TAPS) is a
national non-profit organization made up of and providing services
to those who have lost a loved one in the line of military duty to
America. TAPS offers peer support, crisis intervention (on call 24
hours a day), case workers and grief counseling referrals to help
families and military personnel cope and recover.

Widowed Persons Service
4270 Chicago Dr., SW, Grandville, MI 49418
(616) 538-0101
WPS is a self-help support group for men and women who have
experienced the loss of a spouse through death. They offer daytime
and evening support group meetings, seminars, social activities and
public education of the widowed experience. They have a directory
of the 270 programs across the country and can refer you to one in
your area. They have two excellent videos on the widowed experience that many hospices have purchased.

References

Perspectives on Loss: When Illness Is Prolonged

Hamovitch, Maurice. (1964). *The Parent and the Fatally Ill Child: A Demonstration of Parent Participation in a Hospital Pediatrics Department.* Duarte, CA: City of Hope Medical Center.

Doka—Chapter 1

Doka, Kenneth J. (1984). "Expectations of Death, Participation in Funeral Arrangements, and Grief Adjustment." *Omega,* 15: 119–130.

Doka, Kenneth J. (1989). *Disenfranchised Grief: Recognizing Hidden Sorrow.* Lexington, MA: Lexington Books.

Doka, Kenneth J. (1993). *Living with Life-Threatening Illness: A Guide for Patients, Their Families and Caregivers.* Lexington, MA: Lexington Books.

Doka, Kenneth J., ed. (1995). *Living with Grief: After Sudden Loss.* Washington, D.C.: Taylor & Francis.

Lewis, C.S. (1961). *A Grief Observed.* New York: Bantam.

Rando, Therese A. (1983). "An Investigation of Grief and Adaptation in Parents Whose Children Have Died from Cancer." *Journal of Pediatric Psychology,* 8: 3–20.

Sanders, Catherine. (1983). "Effects of Sudden vs. Chronic Illness on Bereavement Outcome." *Omega,* 13: 227–241.

Sontag, Susan. (1978). *Illness as Metaphor.* New York: McGraw-Hill.

Davies—Chapter 2

Barzelai, L.P. (1981). "Evaluation of a Home-based Hospice." *Journal of Family Practice,* 12: 241–245.

Davies, B., Chekryn-Reimer, J., Brown, P. and Martens, N. (1995). *Fading Away: The Experience of Transition in Families with Terminal Illness.* Amityville, N.Y.: Baywood Publishing Company, Inc.

Lack, S.A. and Buckingham, R.W. (1978). *First American Hospice: Three Years of Home Care.* New Haven: Hospice Inc..

Parkes, C.M. (1985). "Terminal care: Home, hospital or hospice." *Lancet,* 1: 115–117.

Sanders, C.M. (1982-83). "Effects of Sudden vs. Chronic Illness Death on Bereavement Outcome." *Omega,* 13, 3: 227–241.

Steele, L.L. (1990). "The Death Surround: Factors Influencing the Grief Experience for Survivors." *Oncology Nursing Forum,* 17, 2:235–241.

Yancey, D., Greger, H.A., and Coburn, P. (1990). "Determinants of Grief Resolution in Cancer Death." *Journal of Palliative Care.* 6, 4: 24–31.

Rando—Chapter 3

American Psychiatric Association. (1994). *Diagnostic and Statistical Manual of Mental Disorders* (4th ed.). Washington, D.C.

Attig, T. (1996). *How We Grieve: Relearning the World.* New York: Oxford University Press.

Bowlby, J. (1980). *Attachment and Loss: Vol. 3. Loss: Sadness and Depression.* New York: Basic Books, Inc.

Festinger, L. (1957). *A Theory of Cognitive Dissonance.* Stanford, CA: Stanford University Press.

Gerber, I. (1974). "Anticipatory Bereavement." In B. Schoenberg, A. Carr, A. Kutscher, D. Peretz, and I. Goldberg (Eds.), *Anticipatory Grief.* New York: Columbia University Press.

Horowitz, M. (1986). *Stress Response Syndromes (2nd ed.).* Northvale, N.J.: Jason Aronson.

Janoff-Bulman, R. (1985). "The Aftermath of Victimization: Rebuilding Shattered Assumptions." In C. Figley (Ed.), *Trauma and Its Wake: The Study and Treatment of Post-traumatic Stress Disorder.* New York: Brunner/Mazel.

Lindemann, E. (1944). "Symptomatology and Management of Acute Grief." *American Journal of Psychiatry,* 101:141–148.

Neimeyer, R. (1997). "Meaning Reconstruction and the Experience of Chronic Loss." In K.J. Doka (ed.), *Living With Grief When Illness is Prolonged.* Washington, D.C.: Hospice Foundation of America.

Parkes, C. (1988). "Bereavement as a Psychosocial Transition: Processes of Adaptation to Change." *Journal of Social Issues,* 44, 3:53–65.

Rando, T.A. (Ed.) (1986). *Loss and Anticipatory Grief.* Lexington, Mass.: Lexington Books.

Rando, T.A. (1996). "On Treating Those Bereaved by Sudden, Unanticipated Death." *In Session: Psychotherapy In Practice,* 2, 4: 59–71.

Raphael, B. (1981). "Personal Disaster." *Australian and New Zealand Journal of Psychiatry,* 15: 183–198.

Tait, R. and Silver, R. (1989). "Coming to Terms with Major Negative Life Events." In J. Uleman and J. Bargh (Eds.), *Unintended Thought: The Limits of Awareness, Intention, and Control.* New York: Guilford.

Taylor, S. (1983). "Adjustment to Threatening Events: A Theory of Cognitive Adaptation." *American Psychologist,* 38:1161–1173.

Woodfield R. and Viney, L. (1984–1985). "A Personal Construct Approach to the Conjugally Bereaved Woman." *Omega,* 15:1–13.

Price—Chapter 4

Murphy, P.A. and Price, D.M. (1995). "ACT: Taking a Positive Approach to End-of-Life Care." *American Journal of Nursing,* 95, 3:42–43.

The President's Commission for the Study of Ethical Issues in Medicine and Biomedical and Behavioral Research. *Deciding to Forgo Life-Sustaining Treatment.* Washington, DC: U.S. Government Printing Office, 1983.

Price, D.M. and Murphy, P.A. (1994). "DNR: Still Crazy After All These Years." *Journal of Nursing Law,* 1, 3:53–61.

Price, D.M. and Murphy, P.A. (1994). "Tube Feeding and the Ethics of Caring." *Journal of Nursing Law,* 1, 4:53–64.

Solomon, M.Z. (1993). "Decisions Near the End of Life: Professional Views on Life-Sustaining Treatments." *American Journal of Public Health,* 83, 1:14–25.

The SUPPORT Principal Investigators. "A Controlled Trial to Improve Care for Seriously Ill Hospitalized Patients." *Journal of the American Medical Association,* 274, 20:1591–1598.

Lamers—Chapter 5

Christakis, N. et al. (1996). *New England Journal of Medicine,* 335:172–178.

Connor, S. and J. McMaster. (1996). "Hospice, Bereavement Intervention and Use of Health Care Services by Surviving Spouses." *HMO Practice,* 10:1.

Erikson, E. personal communication.

International Work Group on Dying, Death and Bereavement. (1977) *Assumptions and Principles Underlying Standards of Care for the Terminally Ill.* London, Ontario.

Lamers, W. (1990). "Hospice: Enhancing the Quality of Life." *Oncology,* May.

National Hospice Organization. (1996). *Medical Guidelines for Determining Prognosis in Selected Non-Cancer Diseases* (2nd ed.) Arlington, VA.

Raphael, B. (1977). "Preventive Intervention with the Recently Bereaved." *Arch Gen Psychiatry,* 34:1450–1454.

Standards of Hospice Care. Arlington, VA. NHO, 1986.

Stoddard, S. (1992). *The Hospice Movement.* New York: Vintage Press.

Grief, Loss and the Illness Experience

Kubler-Ross, Elisabeth. (1969). *On Death and Dying.* New York: Macmillan.

Corless—Chapter 8

Cherney, P.M., Verhey, M.P. (1996). "Grief Among Gay Men Associated with Multiple Losses from AIDS." *Death Studies,* 20:115–132.

Doka, K.J. (1989). *Disenfranchised Grief: Recognizing Hidden Sorrow.* Lexington, MA: Lexington Books.

Mims, B. (1994). "A Diary of Dying and Living." In I.B. Corless, B.B. Germino, M. Pittman*, Dying, Death, and Bereavement-Theoretical Perspectives and Other Ways of Knowing.* Boston: Jones and Bartlett Publishers, 383–408.

Sanders, C.M. (1989). *Grief: The Mourning After.* New York: John Wiley.

Shilts, R. (1987). *And the Band Played On.* New York: Penguin Books.

Williams/Moretta—Chapter 9

American Psychiatric Association (1994). *Diagnostic and statistical manual of mental disorders* (4th ed.). Washington, D.C.

Anderson, H. (1986). "Therapeutic impasses: A breakdown in conversation." Unpublished manuscript, Houston Galveston Institute, Galveston, TX.

Anderson, H. and Goolishian, H. (1988). "Human systems as linguistic systems: Some preliminary and evolving ideas about the implications for clinical theory." *Family Process,* 27, 371–393.

Anderson, H. and Goolishian H. (1991). "A Collaborative Language Systems Approach." Presented at the May Narrative and Psychotherapy Conference, Houston, TX.

Aronson, M. K. (1988). "Caring for the Dementia Patient." In M.K. Aronson (Ed.) *Understanding Alzheimer's Disease: What It Is, How to Cope with It, Future Directions.* New York: Charles Schribner's Sons.

Austrom, M. G., and Hendrie, H. C. (1990). "Death of the Personality: The Grief Response of the Alzheimer's Disease Family Caregiver," *The American Journal of Alzheimer's Care and Related Disorders and Research,* March/April, 16–27.

Biever, J. L., Gardner, G. T. and Bobele, M. (1995). "Postmodern Perspectives: Social Construction and Family Practice." To be published in Franklin, C. and Jordan C. *Family Practice in Social Work: Interventions and Integrations.* Pacific Grove, CA: Brooks/Cole.

Cohen, D. and Eisdorfer, C. (1986). *The Loss of Self: A family Resource for the Care of Alzheimer's Disease and Related Disorders.* New York: W.W. Norton and Co.

Collins, C., Liken, M., King, S., and Kokinakis, C. (1993). "Loss and Grief among Family Caregivers of Relatives with Dementia." *Qualitative Health Research,* 3:2, 236–253.

Darris, P. (1988). "Alzheimer's Disease and Related Disorders: An Overview." In M.K. Aronson (Ed.) *Understanding Alzheimer's Disease: What It Is, How to Cope with It, Future Directions.* New York: Charles Schribner's Sons.

Doka, K. (1989). *Disenfranchised Grief: Recognizing Hidden Sorrow.* Lexington, MA: Lexington Books.

Doka, K. (1993). *Living with Life-threatening Illness: A Guide for Patients, their Families, and Caregivers.* Lexington, MA: Lexington Books.

Gergen, K. J. (1985). "The Social Construction Movement in Modern Psychology." *American Psychologist,* 40: 266–275.

Hoffman, L. (1990). "Constructing Realities: An Art of Lenses." *Family Process,* 29, 1:1–12.

Keizer, J., and Feins, L.C. (1991). "Intervention Strategies to Use in Counseling Families of Demented Patients." *Journal of Gerontological Social Work,* 17: 201–216.

Mace, N. L., and Rabins, P. V. (1981). *The 36-hour Day: A Family Guide to Caring for Persons with Alzheimer's Disease, Related Dementing Illnesses, and Memory Loss in Later Life.* Baltimore: The Johns Hopkins University Press.

Manning, D. (1983). *When Loves Gets Tough: The Nursing Home Decision.* Hereford, Texas: In-Sight Books, Ind.

Parry, A. and Doan, R. E. (1994). *Story Re-visions: Narrative Therapy in the Postmodern World.* New York: The Guilford Press.

Rosenblatt, P. C. (1994*). Metaphors of Family Systems Theory — Toward New Constructions.* New York: The Guilford Press.

Shotter, J. (1992). "Social Constructionism and Realism: Adequacy or Accuracy?" *Theory and Psychology,* 2: 175–182.

Walker, R. J., E.C. Pomeroy, J.S. McNeil, and C. Franklin. (1994). "Anticipatory Grief and Alzheimer's Disease: Strategies for Intervention." *Journal of Gerontological Social Work,* 22: 3–4, 21-39.

Wyne, L. C., Weber, T. T. and McDaniel, S. H. (1986). "The Road from Family Therapy to Systems Consultation." In L. Wynne, S. McDaniel and T. Weber (Eds.), *Systems Consultation.* New York: The Guilford Press.

Paths to Healing

Martin, Terry and Kenneth J. Doka. (1995). "Masculine Grief.*"* In K. Doka, (Ed.), *Living With Grief: After Sudden Loss.* Washington, D.C.: Taylor and Francis, 865–892.

Corr—Chapter 10

Corr, C. A. (1995). "Children's Understandings of Death: Striving to Understand Death." In K. J. Doka (Ed.), *Children Mourning, Mourning Children.* Washington, DC: Hospice Foundation of America, 3–16.

Corr, C. A., and Balk, D. E. (Eds.). (1996). *Handbook of Adolescent Death and Bereavement.* New York: Springer.

Corr, C. A., and Corr, D. M. (Eds.). (1996). *Handbook of Childhood Death and Bereavement.* New York: Springer.

Corr, C. A., Nabe, C. M., and Corr, D. M. (1997). *Death and Dying, Life and Living* (2nd ed.). Pacific Grove, CA: Brooks/Cole.

Doka, K. J. (1996). "The Cruel Paradox: Children Who Are Living with Life-threatening Illnesses." In C. A. Corr and D. M. Corr (Eds.), *Handbook of Childhood Death and Bereavement.* New York: Springer, 89–105.

Erikson, E. (1963). *Childhood and Society* (2nd ed.). New York: Norton.

Erikson, E. (1968). *Identity: Youth and Crisis.* London: Faber and Faber.

Fox, S. S. (1988). *Good grief: Helping groups of children when a friend dies.* Boston: The New England Association for the Education of Young Children.

Kastenbaum, R. (1977). "Death and Development Through the Lifespan." In. H. Feifel (Ed.), *New Meanings of Death.* New York: McGraw-Hill, 17–45.

Katzenbach, J. (1986). *The Traveler.* New York: Putnam's.

Neimeyer—Chapter 12

Attig, T. (1991). "The Importance of Conceiving of Grief as an Active Process." *Death Studies,* 15: 393.

Attig, T. (1996). *How We Grieve: Relearning the World.* London: Oxford University Press.

Bowlby, J. (1980). *Attachment and Loss: Vol. 3. Loss: Sadness and Depression.* New York: Basic Books.

Braun, M. and Berg, D. H. (1994). "Meaning Reconstruction in the Experience of Parental Bereavement." *Death Studies,* 18, 105–129.

Canine, J. D. (1990). *I Can, I Will.* Birmingham, Mich.: Ball Publishers.

Corr, C. A. (1993). "Coping with Dying: Lessons that We Should and Should Not Learn from the Work of Elisabeth Kubler-Ross." *Death Studies,* 17: 69–83.

Davidson, G. W. (1979). "Hospice Care for the Dying." In H. Wass (Ed.) *Dying: Facing the Facts* (1st ed.). Washington DC: McGraw-Hill.

Doka, K. J. and Morgan, J. D. (1993). *Death and Spirituality.* Amityville, NY: Baywood.

Downe-Wambolt, B., Tamlyn, D. (in press). "An International Survey of Death Education Trends in Faculties of Nursing and Medicine." *Death Studies.*

Engel, G. (1964). "Grief and Grieving." *American Journal of Nursing,* 64: 93–98.

Feigenberg, L. (1980). *Terminal Care: Friendship Contracts with Dying Cancer Patients.* New York: Brunner/Mazel.

Janoff-Bulman, R. (1989). "Assumptive Worlds and the Stress of Traumatic Events: Applications of the Schema Construct." *Social Cognition,* 7: 113–116.

Janoff-Bulman, R. (1992). *Shattered Assumptions: Towards a New Psychology of Trauma.* New York: Free Press.

Harvey, J. H. (1996). *Embracing Their Memory.* Boston: Allyn and Bacon.

Howard, G. S. (1991). "Culture Tales: A Narrative Approach to Thinking, Cross-cultural Psychology, and Psychotherapy." *American Psychologist,* 46: 187–197.

Kelly, G. K. (1955). *The Psychology of Personal Constructs.* New York: Norton.

Kelly, G.A. (1973). "Fixed Role Therapy." In R. M. Jerjevich (Ed.), *Direct Psychotherapy.* Coral Gables, FL: University of Miami Press, 394–422.

Klass, D., Silverman, P. R. and S. Nickman (Eds.) (1996). *Continuing Bonds: New Understandings of Grief.* Washington, DC: Taylor and Francis.

Kubler-Ross, E. (1969). *On Death and Dying.* New York: Macmillan.

Lindemann, E. (1944). "Symptomology and Management of Acute Grief." *American Journal of Psychiatry,* 101: 141–148.

Mahoney, M. J. (1991). *Human Change Processes.* New York: Basic Books.

Mair, J. M. M. (1977). "The Community of Self." In D. Bannister (Ed.) *New Perspectives in Personal Construct Theory.* London: Academic Press, 125–150.

Milo, E. M. (1997). "Maternal Responses to the Life and Death of a Child with a Developmental Disability: A Story of Hope." *Death Studies,* in press.

Neimeyer, R. A. (1987). "An Orientation to Personal Construct Therapy." In R. A. Neimeyer and G. J. Neimeyer (Eds.). *Personal Construct Therapy Casebook.* New York: Springer, 3–19.

Neimeyer, R. A. (1993). "Constructivism and the Cognitive Psychotherapies: Some Conceptual and Strategic Contrasts." *Journal of Cognitive Psychotherapy,* 7: 159–171.

Neimeyer, R. A. (1994). "The Threat Index and Related Methods." In R. A. Neimeyer (Ed.), *Death Anxiety Handbook: Research, Instrumentation, and Application.* Washington DC: Taylor and Francis.

Neimeyer, R. A. (1995a). "Constructivist Psychotherapies: Features, Foundations, and Future Directions." In R. A. Neimeyer and M. J. Mahoney (Eds.). *Constructivism in Psychotherapy.* Washington DC: American Psychological Association, 11–38.

Neimeyer, R. A. (1995b). "Limits and Lessons of Constructivism: Some Critical Reflections." *Journal of Constructivist Psychology,* 8, 339–361.

Neimeyer, R. A. (1995c). "Client Generated Narratives in Psychotherapy." In R. A. Neimeyer and M. J. Mahoney (Eds.) *Constructivism in Psychotherapy.* Washington DC: American Psychological Association, 231–246.

Neimeyer, R.A., Keesee, N.J. and Fortner, B.V. (1997). "Loss and Meaning Reconstruction: Propositions and Procedures." In S. Rubin, R.

Malkinson and E. Wiztum (Eds.), *Traumatic and Non-traumatic Loss and Bereavement: Clinical Theory and Practice.* Madison, CT: Psychosocial Press.

Neimeyer, R. A. and M. J. Mahoney (Eds.). (1995). *Constructivism in Psychotherapy.* Washington, D.C.: American Psychological Association.

Neimeyer, R. A. and Stewart, A. E. (1996). "Trauma, Healing, and the Narrative Emplotment of Loss." *Families in Society: The Journal of Contemporary Human Services,* 77: 360–375.

Parkes, C. M. (1988). "Bereavement as a Psychosocial Transition: Processes of Adaptation to Change." *Journal of Social Issues,* 44: 53–65.

Polkinghorne, D. E. (1991). "Narrative and Self-concept." *Journal of Narrative and Life History,* 1: 135–153.

Polkinghorne, D. E. (1992). "Postmodern Epistemology of Practice." In S. Kvale (Ed.), *Psychology and Postmodernism.* London: Sage, 146–165.

Rando, T. A. (1995). "Grief and Mourning: Accommodating to Loss." In H. Wass and R. A. Neimeyer (Eds.). *Dying: Facing the Facts,* (3rd ed.). Washington, D.C.: Taylor and Francis, 211–241.

Rubin, S. S. (1993). "The Death of a Child is Forever: The Life Course Impact of Child Loss." In M. S. Stroebe, W. Stroebe and R. O. Hansson (Eds.), *Handbook of Bereavement.* New York: Cambridge University Press.

Shneidman, E. (1980). *Voices of Death.* New York: Harper and Row.

Sluzki, C. E. (1991). Foreword. In F. Walsh and M. McGoldrick (Eds.), *Living Beyond Loss.* New York: Norton, vi–viii.

Stroebe, M. (1992–93). "Coping with Bereavement: A Review of the Grief Work Hypothesis." *Omega,* 26: 19–42.

Stroebe, W., and Stroebe, M. (1994). "Is Grief Universal? Cultural Variations in the Emotional Reaction to Loss." In R. Fulton and R. Bendiksen (Eds.), *Death and Identity* (3rd ed.) Philadelphia: Charles Press, 177–209.

Viney, L. L. (1991). "The Personal Construct Theory of Death and Loss: Toward a More Individually Oriented Grief Therapy." *Death Studies,* 15: 139–155.

Walsh, F. and McGoldrick, M. (Eds.) (1991). *Living Beyond Loss.* New York: Norton.

White, M. and Epston, D. (1990). *Narrative Means to Therapeutic Ends.* New York: Norton.

Wolowelsky, J. B. (1996). "Communal and Individual Mourning Dynamics within Traditional Jewish Law." *Death Studies,* 20: 469–480.

Worden, J. W. (1991). *Grief Counseling and Grief Therapy.* New York: Sage.

Wortman, C. B., and Silver, R. C. (1989). "The myths of coping with loss." *Journal of Consulting and Clinical Psychology.* 57: 349–357.

Zulli/Weeks—Chapter 13

Callanan, M. and P. Kelly. (1992). *Final Gifts.* New York: Poseidon Press.

Doka, K. (1989). *Disenfranchised Grief: Recognizing Hidden Sorrow.* Lexington, MA: Lexington Press.

Eliot, T. S. (1943). *Four Quarters.* New York, NY: Harcourt, Brace and World.

Houston, J.(1987). *The Search for the Beloved.* Los Angeles, CA: Jeremy Tarcher.

Imber-Black, E. and J. Roberts. (1992) *Rituals for Our Times: Celebrating, Healing, and Changing Our Lives and Our Relationships.* New York: Harper Perennial.

Manning, D. (1995). "The clergy factor." *The Dodge Magazine,* January– February: 4–5.

Paladin, L. (1991) *Ceremonies for Change: Creating Personal Ritual to Heal Life's Hurts.* Walpole, NH: Stillpoint Publishing International.

Rando, T. (1984) *Grief, Dying, and Death — Clinical Interventions for Caregivers.* Champaign, IL: Research Press.

Sanders, C. (1989) *Grief, the Mourning After.* New York: John Wiley and Sons.

Conclusion

Borysenko, Joan. (1996). Fourth Annual Governing Board Lecture, Morristown Memorial Health Foundation, Morristown, New Jersey.

Frankl, Victor. (1984). *Man's Search for Meaning.* New York: Simon and Schuster.

Oliver, Mary. (1992). *New and Selected Poems.* Boston: Beacon Press.

Biographical Information

Inge B. Corless, R.N., Ph.D., F.A.A.N, Associate Professor of Nursing, is the Director of the HIV/AIDS Specialization at the MGH Institute of Health Professions in Boston, MA. She has written a number of publications about AIDS and health care, and has served as editor on several books about dying, death, and bereavement.

Charles A. Corr is one of America's leaders in death education, and Professor of Philosophy at Southern Illinois University at Edwardsville. He is the former Chairperson of the International Work Group on Death, Dying, and Bereavement, and the author of many books on children and death, hospice, and Sudden Infant Death Syndrome (SIDS).

Joyce Davidson, a former magazine editor and free-lance writer, is pursuing studies in counseling and thanatology with Ken Doka at the College of New Rochelle.

Betty Davies, R.N., Ph.D., has worked as a nurse specializing in the areas of death, dying, and bereavement for over twenty years. She is a Founding member of the Board of HUGS Children's Hospice Society. She has conducted several studies in palliative care and co-authored a book focusing on the families of both child and adult patients. Dr. Davies has served on the Boards of the International Work Group on Death, Dying, and Bereavement, and the Association for Death Education and Counseling.

Kenneth J. Doka, Ph.D., is a Professor of Gerontology at the College of New Rochelle. Dr. Doka is the associate editor of the journal *Omega* and editor of *Journeys,* a newsletter for the bereaved. He has served as a consultant to medical, nursing, and hospice organizations including the Hospice Foundation of America, and to businesses, educational and social service agencies. In March 1993, he was elected President of the Association for Death Education and Counseling. In 1995 he was elected to the Board of the International Work Group on Dying, Death and Bereavement, and elected Chair in 1997. Dr. Doka is an ordained Lutheran clergyman.

Annette Dula, Ed.D., is a senior research associate at the Center for the Study of Race in America at the University of Colorado at Boulder, a Fellow at the University of Chicago Center for Clinical Medical Ethics, and has taught ethics at the University of Massachusetts Medical Center. She has written and spoken extensively on health care ethics from an African American perspective, and served on the bioethics committee of President Clinton's Health Task Force.

Earl A. Grollman, D.D., is a rabbi, a pioneer in the fields of death education and crisis intervention and the author of 24 books about death and dying. He speaks frequently at conferences and symposia, and is often called to scenes of traumatic injury and death as a counselor to both victims' families and to caregivers.

Stephen P. Hersh, M.D., F.A.P.A., is a psychiatrist and director of the Medical Illness Counseling Center, a nonprofit clinic dealing with the chronically and terminally ill and their families. He is a Clinical Professor of Psychiatry, Behavioral Sciences and Pediatrics at George Washington University School of Medicine, a consult to the National Cancer Institute, as well as a member of the medical staff of the Clinical Center, National Institutes of Health.

William M. Lamers, Jr., M.D., is a founding father of the American Hospice Movement and a pioneer in the concept of hospice as home care. Dr. Lamers is the author of many books on hospice care, as well as grief and bereavement, and works as a consultant in the areas of hospice, palliative care, and pain management.

Brenda Moretta, Ph.D., is currently an instructor and undergraduate program director in psychology at Our Lady of the Lake University in San Antonio, Texas. She has worked with cancer and Alzheimer's patients and their families for 15 years. Dr. Moretta teaches and conducts training seminars for hospital and hospice personnel, and is a member of the Association for Death Education and Counseling.

Robert A. Neimeyer, Ph.D., is a Professor in the Department of Psychology at the University of Memphis. He has published 14 books and numerous articles and collaborations on death and dying, and is the editor of *Death Studies,* series editor for the Taylor and Francis *Series on Death, Dying, and Bereavement,* and President of the Association for Death Education and Counseling.

David M. Price, M. Div., Ph.D., has taught professional ethics at New Jersey Medical School in Newark since 1979. Since 1992 he has also been the hospital ethicist at Saint Barnabas Medical Center in Livingston, NJ. He is a founding member of ethics committees in five hospitals, several nursing homes and a hospice. Dr. Price is a director of New Jersey Health Decisions and a consultant to the NJ Board of Medical Examiners. His articles appear in medical, nursing, ethics and legal journals.

Therese A. Rando, Ph.D., is a clinical psychologist, and the founder and clinical director of the Institute for the Study and Treatment of Loss in Warwick, Rhode Island. The Institute and her private practice focus on providing psychotherapy, training, supervision and consultation in loss and grief, traumatic stress, and the psychosocial care of the chronically and terminally ill. Dr. Rando has written and edited numerous books and articles pertaining to the clinical aspects of thanatology.

O. Duane Weeks, Ph.D., has been a licensed funeral director and embalmer for over 30 years and owns four funeral homes in the state of Washington. His interest in death education and grief-related issues led him to a doctorate in sociology from the University of Minnesota. Dr. Weeks is the Director of the New England Institute of Funeral Service of Mount Ida College in Newton Centre, Massachusetts.

Carol Williams, M.S., received her degree in counseling psychology with a specialization in Marriage and Family Therapy, and is currently finishing her Psy.D. at Our Lady of the Lake University in San Antonio, Texas. She has extensive experience in long-term nursing care and is a private geriatric consultant in specialized memory impaired units. Ms. Williams is currently a Crisis Response Team Counselor with the San Antonio Police Department, and conducts training seminars related to her clinical work and research.

Alice Parsons Zulli is an ordained minister, and founder and Director of *Beyond Loss,* a bereavement ministry. She is a Certified Thanatologist, Grief Counselor, and Bereavement Support Educator, and a member of the National Hospice Organization and the American Association of Suicidology. Rev. Zulli is a support Chaplain at Glendale Adventist Medical Center in Glendale, California, and facilitates support groups, educates professionals in bereavement facilitating, is an active conference speaker, and has a large private practice.

DATE DUE
